KU-412-904

Made from scratch

VEGETARIAN

EVERYDAY EASY HOME COOKING

This edition published by Parragon Books Ltd in 2014
LOVE FOOD is an imprint of Parragon Books Ltd

Parragon Books Ltd
Chartist House
15–17 Trim Street
Bath BA1 1HA, UK
www.parragon.com/lovefood

Copyright © Parragon Books Ltd 2012 – 2014

LOVE FOOD and the accompanying heart device is a registered trademark of
Parragon Books Ltd in Australia, the UK, USA, India and the EU.

All rights reserved. No part of this publication may be reproduced, stored
in a retrieval system or transmitted, in any form or by any means, electronic,
mechanical, photocopying, recording or otherwise, without the prior permission
of the copyright holder.

ISBN 978-1-4723-2995-0

Printed in China

Cover photography by Ian Garlick
Design by Geoff Borin
New photography by Noel Murphy
New home economy by Sue Henderson
New recipes by Teresa Goldfinch
Introduction and notes by Sarah Bush
Edited by Fiona Biggs
Nutritional analysis by Fiona Hunter

Notes for the Reader
This book uses both metric and imperial measurements. Follow the same
units of measurement throughout; do not mix metric and imperial. All spoon
measurements are level: teaspoons are assumed to be 5 ml, and tablespoons
are assumed to be 15 ml. Unless otherwise stated, milk is assumed to be full fat,
eggs and individual vegetables are medium, and pepper is freshly ground black
pepper. Unless otherwise stated, all root vegetables should be peeled prior
to using.

Garnishes, decorations and serving suggestions are all optional and not
necessarily included in the recipe ingredients or method. Any optional
ingredients and seasoning to taste are not included in the nutritional analysis. The
times given are an approximate guide only. Preparation times differ according
to the techniques used by different people and the cooking times may also vary
from those given. Optional ingredients, variations or serving suggestions have not
been included in the time calculations.

Vegetarians should be aware that some of the ready-made ingredients used in the
recipes in this book may contain animal products. Always check the packaging
before use.

Contents

Introduction 4

Soups & Starters 6

Salads & Light Meals 36

Main Meals 66

Accompaniments 96

Index 126

Introduction

There are many misconceptions surrounding a vegetarian diet but, put simply, someone following this regime removes meat, fish and poultry from their meals and replaces them with vegetables, grains, pasta, beans, lentils, fresh fruit and nuts. Today, more and more people are considering replacing two or three main meals a week with a vegetarian alternative – others may have decided to convert totally.

Equally, almost all of us will know someone within our family circle or friends who is a vegetarian, so it is important to understand the basic principles when cooking for them.

Benefits of a vegetarian diet

You may be surprised, but the western diet used to consist mainly of cereals, pulses and vegetables because most people grew their own food or bought it locally and meat or poultry was considered a luxury only for special occasions. This high fibre, low-fat, low-sugar, low-salt diet was far healthier for us and illnesses that are common today were rare. The availability of mass-produced processed foods has made our lives easier, but is more of a concern for our health.

New inspirations

Today, being vegetarian is much easier than it was in the past. For a start there are so many more ingredients available in our supermarkets and speciality stores. Many other cultures, whose diets tend to revolve more around vegetables, are increasingly influential and we can draw on spicy seasonings from Asia, robust flavours from the Mediterranean and exciting grain dishes from Africa. Travelling to holiday destinations further afield has encouraged us to sample the unfamiliar and given us a desire to cook similar dishes back home. Restaurants are more aware of the changing trends of eating and include meatless choices on their menus which are enjoyed by vegetarians and non-vegetarians alike.

Explore your local ethnic food stores to find a range of exciting ingredients and spices.

Vegetarians and the environment

The range of fresh produce today is staggering and growers and producers are constantly tempting us with new foods. Growing our own vegetables, fruit and herbs is more popular and farmers' markets spring up regularly in towns all over the country. By shopping locally we support small businesses and help lessen our environmental impact. A supply of fresh, organically grown vegetables, fruit and salads are just on our doorstep – a boon to the vegetarian diet. Sometimes you pay a premium for this as harvesting is done on a smaller scale and often by hand rather than using large-scale machinery, however, if you're not buying more expensive meat and poultry items each week, the saving is transferred.

Vegetarians and vegans

When considering the pros and cons of changing your eating habits you should investigate the various approaches to vegetarian food. Some people consider themselves vegetarian yet they eat fish and others will eat chicken. Then there are those who follow the vegan diet and only eat foods of plant origin and therefore don't eat milk, butter, eggs, or even honey. Whichever route you choose, variety is the key to maintaining a balanced diet.

The recipes included in this book do not include any meat or fish products, but may contain dairy such as eggs, milk and cheese, so are not suitable for vegans, unless specified.

Pea & Herb Soup with Basil Oil *8*

Aubergine Pâté *10*

Spicy Courgette Soup with Rice & Lime *12*

Feta, Lemon & Herb Dip *14*

Vegetable & Corn Chowder *16*

Spicy Avocado Dip *18*

Spicy Lentil Soup *20*

Mini Roast Vegetable Skewers *22*

Roast Squash Soup with Cheese Toasties *24*

Blue Cheese & Herb Pâté *26*

White Bean Soup *28*

Vegetable Pakoras *30*

Thai Vermicelli Soup *32*

Grilled Halloumi Kebabs on Fennel & White Bean Salad *34*

Soups & Starters

Pea & Herb Soup with Basil Oil

 SERVES 4

 PREP TIME:
15 minutes
plus chilling

 COOKING TIME:
15–20 minutes

nutritional information
per serving   277 kcals, 22g fat, 8g sat fat, 4g total sugars, 0.2g salt

This elegant soup is delicious hot or chilled.

INGREDIENTS

30 g/1 oz butter
6 spring onions, chopped
1 celery stick, finely chopped
375 g/13 oz frozen peas or fresh shelled peas
700 ml/1¼ pints vegetable stock
2 tbsp chopped fresh dill
1 tbsp snipped fresh chives
35 g/1¼ oz rocket leaves
2 tbsp crème fraîche
salt and pepper
bread sticks, to serve

basil oil
1 x 30-g/1-oz bunch of basil
200 ml/7 fl oz olive oil

1. Melt the butter in a saucepan over a medium heat. Add the spring onions and celery, cover and cook for 5 minutes until soft. Add the peas and stock, bring to the boil and simmer for 10 minutes. Remove from the heat. Cover and leave to cool for 20 minutes.

2. To make the basil oil, remove the stems from the basil and discard. Place the leaves in a food processor with half the oil and blend to a purée. Add the remaining oil and blend again. Transfer to a small bowl.

3. Add the dill, chives and rocket to the soup. Blend with a hand-held blender until smooth. Stir in the crème fraîche. If serving warm, heat through gently without boiling, then season to taste.

4. Ladle into four warmed bowls and drizzle with the basil oil. Serve immediately, with bread sticks on the side. If serving chilled, leave to cool completely, then chill in the refrigerator for at least 1 hour before checking the seasoning and serving.

COOK'S NOTE
Any leftover
basil oil can
be stored in
the refrigerator
for 3-4 days
and used for
drizzling over
salads or ciabatta
or tossing with
pasta.

Aubergine Pâté

 SERVES 6   PREP TIME: 10 minutes plus cooling   COOKING TIME: 1¼ hours

nutritional information per serving	73 kcals, 7.5g fat, 1g sat fat, 1g total sugars, trace salt

Also known as Poor Man's Caviar because the humble aubergine when prepared this way tastes so delicious!

INGREDIENTS

2 large aubergines
4 tbsp extra virgin olive oil
2 garlic cloves, very finely chopped
4 tbsp lemon juice
salt and pepper
2 tbsp roughly chopped fresh flat-leaf parsley, to garnish
6 crisp breads, to serve

1. Preheat the oven to 180°C/350°F/Gas Mark 4. Score the skins of the aubergines with the point of a sharp knife, without piercing the flesh, and place them on a baking sheet. Bake for 1¼ hours, or until soft.

2. Remove the aubergines from the oven and leave until cool enough to handle. Cut them in half and, using a spoon, scoop out the flesh into a bowl. Mash the flesh thoroughly.

3. Gradually beat in the olive oil then stir in the garlic and lemon juice. Season to taste with salt and pepper. Cover with clingfilm and store in the refrigerator until required. Sprinkle with the parsley and serve with crisp breads.

1
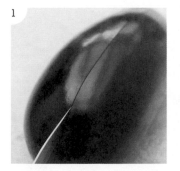

2

3

COOK'S NOTE
Makes a great dip too, served with sticks of carrot, celery and pepper.

Spicy Courgette Soup with Rice & Lime

 SERVES 4 　　 PREP TIME: 10 minutes 　　 COOKING TIME: 20 minutes

nutritional information per serving	195 kcals, 6g fat, 0.7g sat fat, 0.8g total sugars, 1g salt

A squeeze of lime added to this light, fresh tasting soup makes all the difference.

INGREDIENTS

2 tbsp vegetable oil

4 garlic cloves, thinly sliced

1–2 tbsp mild red chilli powder

¼ –½ tsp ground cumin

1.5 litres/2¾ pints vegetable stock

2 courgettes, cut into bite-sized chunks

4 tbsp long-grain rice

salt and pepper

fresh oregano sprigs, to garnish

lime wedges, to serve

1. Heat the oil in a heavy-based saucepan. Add the garlic and cook for 2 minutes, or until softened. Add the chilli powder and cumin and cook over a medium–low heat for 1 minute.

2. Stir in the stock, courgettes and rice, then cook over a medium–high heat for 10 minutes, or until the courgettes are just tender and the rice is cooked through. Season to taste with salt and pepper.

3. Ladle into warmed bowls, garnish with oregano sprigs and serve immediately with lime wedges.

SOMETHING
DIFFERENT

Use a combination
of green and
yellow courgettes
for extra colour.

Feta, Lemon & Herb Dip

 SERVES 5

 PREP TIME:
5 minutes
plus chilling

 COOKING TIME:
No cooking

nutritional information per serving	117 kcals, 10g fat, 5g sat fat, 0.3g total sugars, 1g salt

This quickly made dip is also lovely served as an accompaniment to vegetable kebabs and jacket potatoes.

INGREDIENTS

150 g/5½ oz vegetarian low-fat soft cheese

3 tbsp water

1 tbsp olive oil

100 g/3½ oz vegetarian feta cheese, crumbled

1 large lemon

3 tbsp roughly chopped fresh mint

3 tbsp roughly chopped fresh dill

pepper

a selection of vegetable crudités, to serve

1. Place the soft cheese, water and oil in a food processor and process until smooth. Add the feta cheese and process briefly to combine, but make sure there are still some small lumps remaining. Transfer to a bowl.

2. Pare the zest from the lemon using a zester. Stir the zest into the dip with the mint and dill. Season with pepper. Cover and chill for at least 30 minutes to develop the flavours. Serve with a selection of vegetable crudités for dipping.

1

1

2

GET AHEAD
The dip and crudités can be prepared a day ahead and kept in the refrigerator.

Vegetable & Corn Chowder

 SERVES 4　　 PREP TIME: 10 minutes　　 COOKING TIME: 25–30 minutes

nutritional information per serving	363 kcals, 16g fat, 8g sat fat, 14g total sugars, 0.8g salt

Chowder is traditionally from New England in the United States and is another name for a thick, hearty soup.

INGREDIENTS

1 tbsp vegetable oil

1 red onion, diced

1 red pepper, deseeded and diced

3 garlic cloves, crushed

300 g/10½ oz potatoes, diced

2 tbsp plain flour

600 ml/1 pint milk

300 ml/10 fl oz vegetable stock

50 g/1¾ oz broccoli florets

300 g/10½ oz canned sweetcorn, drained

75 g/2¾ oz vegetarian Cheddar cheese, grated

salt and pepper

1. Heat the oil in a large saucepan. Add the onion, red pepper, garlic and potatoes and sauté over a low heat, stirring frequently, for 2–3 minutes.

2. Stir in the flour and cook, stirring, for 30 seconds. Gradually stir in the milk and stock.

3. Add the broccoli and sweetcorn. Bring the mixture to the boil, stirring constantly, then reduce the heat and simmer for about 20 minutes, or until all the vegetables are tender.

4. Stir in 50 g/1¾ oz of the cheese until it melts. Season to taste and ladle into warmed bowls. Garnish with the remaining cheese and serve immediately.

1

2

3

GOES WELL WITH
Serve with crusty
sourdough or
wholemeal bread
for a satisfying
lunch.

Spicy Avocado Dip

 SERVES 4   PREP TIME:
10 minutes   COOKING TIME:
No cooking

nutritional information per serving	192 kcals, 19g fat, 4g sat fat, 1g total sugars, trace salt

When choosing avocados for this great tasting dip, go for the crinkly skinned ones which have a better flavour. Check the ripeness too – they should just give slightly when pressed gently with your thumb.

INGREDIENTS

2 large avocados
juice of 1–2 limes
2 large garlic cloves, crushed
1 tsp mild chilli powder,
or to taste, plus extra to garnish
salt and pepper

1. Cut the avocados in half. Remove the stones and skin and discard.

2. Place the avocado flesh in a food processor with the juice of 1 or 2 limes, according to taste. Add the garlic and chilli powder and process until smooth.

3. Season to taste with salt and pepper. Transfer to a serving bowl, garnish with chilli powder and serve.

1

2

2

SOMETHING
DIFFERENT
Add some diced,
deseeded tomatoes
or cucumber to
the mixture for
added crunch.

Spicy Lentil Soup

 SERVES 4   PREP TIME: 5 minutes   COOKING TIME: 35–40 minutes

nutritional information per serving	235 kcals, 6g fat, 0.8g sat fat, 2g total sugars, trace salt

Just the recipe when you want a simple soup packed with great flavours.

INGREDIENTS

1 litre/1¾ pints water

250 g/9 oz toor dhal or chana dhal

1 tsp paprika

½ tsp chilli powder

½ tsp ground turmeric

2 tbsp ghee or vegetable oil

1 fresh green chilli, deseeded and finely chopped

1 tsp cumin seeds

3 curry leaves, roughly torn

1 tsp sugar

salt

1 tsp garam masala, to garnish

1. Bring the water to the boil in a large, heavy-based saucepan. Add the dhal, cover and simmer, stirring occasionally, for 25 minutes.

2. Stir in the paprika, chilli powder and turmeric, re-cover and cook for a further 10 minutes, or until the dhal is tender.

3. Meanwhile, heat the ghee in a small frying pan. Add the chilli, cumin seeds and curry leaves and cook, stirring constantly, for 1 minute.

4. Add the spice mixture to the dhal. Stir in the sugar and season to taste with salt. Ladle into warmed bowls, garnish with garam masala and serve immediately.

FREEZING TIP
If you find a fresh supply of curry leaves it's worth freezing them in a zippered bag to use when you fancy making a dish like this.

Mini Roast Vegetable Skewers

 SERVES 4

 PREP TIME:
10 minutes

 COOKING TIME:
25–30 minutes

nutritional information per serving	135 kcals, 8g fat, 2g sat fat, 10g total sugars, 0.2g salt

Roasting vegetables in the oven brings out their natural sweetness and the pieces stay in neat shapes too.

INGREDIENTS

1 red pepper, deseeded
1 yellow pepper, deseeded
1 large courgette
1 aubergine
2 tbsp olive oil
3 garlic cloves, crushed
salt and pepper

dip
2 tbsp chopped fresh dill
2 tbsp chopped fresh mint
250 ml/9 fl oz natural yogurt

1. Preheat the oven to 200°C/400°F/Gas Mark 6. Cut the vegetables into 2-cm/¾-inch chunks. Place in a roasting tin large enough to hold them in a single layer.

2. Mix the olive oil and garlic together and drizzle over the top. Season well with salt and pepper then toss together. Roast for 25–30 minutes until tender and lightly charred.

3. Meanwhile, stir the dill and mint into the yogurt. Spoon into four serving bowls.

4. When the vegetables are cool enough to handle, divide them between 12 cocktail sticks. Serve warm or cold with the bowls of dip on the side.

1

2

3

BE PREPARED
Cut the vegetables into
chunks in advance and
marinate for several
hours or overnight.

Roast Squash Soup with Cheese Toasties

 SERVES 4   PREP TIME: 20 minutes   COOKING TIME: 1 hour

nutritional information **per serving** | 548 kcals, 26g fat, 13g sat fat, 16g total sugars, 1.4g salt

A comforting, velvety textured soup that's perfect for freezing.

INGREDIENTS

1 kg/2 lb 4 oz butternut squash, cut into small chunks
2 onions, cut into wedges
2 tbsp olive oil
2 garlic cloves, crushed
3–4 fresh thyme sprigs, leaves removed
1 litre/1¾ pints vegetable stock
150 ml/5 fl oz crème fraîche
salt and pepper
snipped fresh chives, to garnish

toasties

1 baguette, thinly sliced diagonally
40 g/1½ oz vegetarian hard cheese, grated

1. Preheat the oven to 190°C/375°F/Gas Mark 5. Place the squash, onions, oil, garlic and thyme leaves in a roasting tin. Toss together and spread out in a single layer. Roast for 50–60 minutes, stirring occasionally, until the vegetables are tender and caramelized in places.

2. Transfer the vegetables to a saucepan. Add half the stock and purée with a hand-held blender until smooth. Alternatively, blend in a food processor, then transfer to a saucepan. Stir in the remaining stock and crème fraîche. Season to taste with salt and pepper, and heat through gently.

3. To make the toasties, preheat the grill to high. Toast the sliced baguette under the preheated grill for 1–2 minutes on each side until pale golden in colour. Sprinkle with the cheese and return to the grill for a further 30–40 seconds until melted and bubbling.

4. Ladle the soup into four warmed bowls and sprinkle with chives to garnish. Serve immediately with the cheese toasties on the side.

Blue Cheese & Herb Pâté

 SERVES 4   PREP TIME: 15 minutes plus chilling   COOKING TIME: 1 minute

| nutritional information per serving | 509 kcals, 42g fat, 25g sat fat, 5g total sugars, 1.3g salt |

If you're stuck for something to serve as a starter or pack for a posh picnic, this pâté is ideal.

INGREDIENTS

150 g/5½ oz vegetarian low-fat soft cheese

350 g/12 oz fromage frais

115 g/4 oz vegetarian blue cheese, crumbled

55 g/2 oz dried cranberries, finely chopped

5 tbsp chopped fresh herbs, such as parsley, chives, dill and tarragon

85 g/3 oz butter

2 tbsp chopped walnuts

granary toast or bread sticks, to serve

1. Beat the soft cheese to soften, then gradually beat in the fromage frais until smooth. Add the blue cheese, cranberries and herbs. Stir together. Spoon the mixture into four 150-ml/5-fl oz ramekins or small dishes and carefully smooth the tops.

2. Clarify the butter by gently heating it in a small saucepan until melted. Skim any foam off the surface and discard. Carefully pour the clear yellow top layer into a small jug, leaving the milky liquid in the pan. The yellow layer is the clarified butter. Discard the liquid left in the pan.

3. Pour a little of the clarified butter over the top of each pâté and sprinkle with the walnuts. Chill for at least 30 minutes until firm. Serve with granary toast.

SOMETHING
DIFFERENT
The blue cheese
can be replaced
with tangy
vegetarian goat's
cheese if you
prefer.

White Bean Soup

 SERVES 4   PREP TIME:
10 minutes
plus soaking    COOKING TIME:
2 hours 20 minutes

nutritional information per serving	384 kcals, 18g fat, 2.5g sat fat, 1.5g total sugars, trace salt

A traditional Italian country soup from Tuscany that's worth starting the day before as the flavours will improve.

INGREDIENTS

175 g/6 oz dried cannellini beans, soaked in cold water to cover overnight

1.5 litres/2¾ pints vegetable stock

115 g/4 oz dried corallini, conchigliette piccole, or other soup pasta

6 tbsp olive oil

2 garlic cloves, finely chopped

4 tbsp chopped fresh flat-leaf parsley

salt and pepper

fresh crusty bread, to serve

1. Drain the soaked beans and place them in a large, heavy-based saucepan. Add the stock and bring to the boil. Partially cover the pan, then reduce the heat and simmer for 2 hours, or until tender.

2. Transfer about half the beans and a little of the stock to a food processor or blender and process to a smooth purée. Return the purée to the pan and stir well to mix. Return to the boil.

3. Add the pasta, return to the boil and cook for 10 minutes, or until tender.

4. Meanwhile, heat 4 tablespoons of the olive oil in a small saucepan. Add the garlic and cook over a low heat, stirring frequently, for 4–5 minutes, or until golden. Stir the garlic mixture into the soup and add the parsley. Season with salt and pepper and ladle into warmed bowls. Drizzle with the remaining olive oil and serve immediately with crusty bread.

1

2

3

GOES WELL WITH
Green salad
leaves tossed
with balsamic
dressing and
topped with
shavings of
cheese.

Vegetable Pakoras

 SERVES 4

 PREP TIME:
20 minutes

 COOKING TIME:
15 minutes

nutritional information
per serving

236 kcals, 12g fat, 1.5g sat fat, 4g total sugars, 0.6g salt

Serve these crunchy vegetable fritters piping hot as a snack or part of an Indian inspired meal.

INGREDIENTS

6 tbsp gram flour
½ tsp salt
1 tsp chilli powder
1 tsp baking powder
1½ tsp white cumin seeds
1 tsp pomegranate seeds
300 ml/10 fl oz water
¼ bunch of fresh coriander,
finely chopped, plus extra
sprigs to garnish

vegetables of your choice
cauliflower, cut into small florets;
onions, cut into rings; potatoes,
sliced; aubergines, sliced; or
fresh spinach leaves
vegetable oil, for deep-frying

1. Sift the gram flour into a large bowl. Add the salt, chilli powder, baking powder, cumin and pomegranate seeds and blend together well. Pour in the water and beat well to form a smooth batter. Add the chopped coriander and mix well, then set aside.

2. Dip the prepared vegetables into the batter, carefully shaking off any excess.

3. Heat enough oil for deep-frying in a wok, deep-fat fryer or a large, heavy-based saucepan until it reaches 180°C/350°F, or until a cube of bread browns in 30 seconds. Using tongs, place the battered vegetables in the oil and deep-fry, in batches, turning once.

4. Repeat this process until all of the batter has been used up. Transfer the battered vegetables to crumpled kitchen paper and drain thoroughly. Garnish with coriander sprigs and serve immediately.

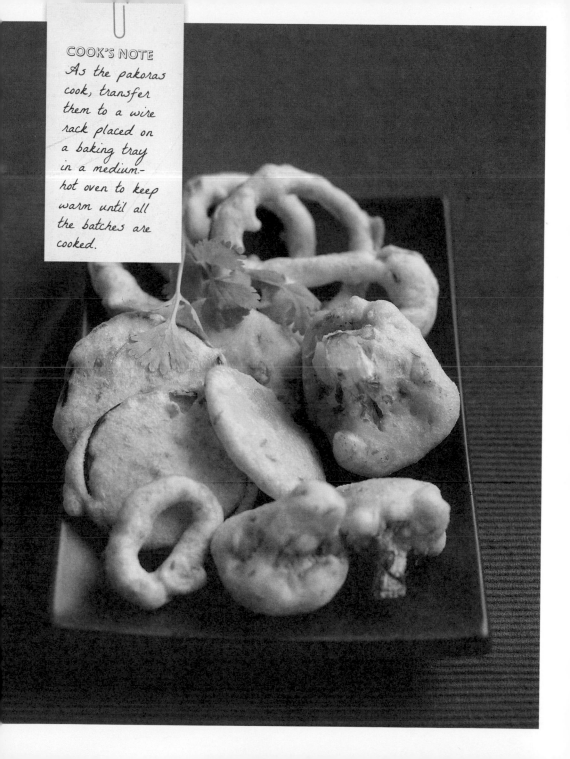

COOK'S NOTE

As the pakoras cook, transfer them to a wire rack placed on a baking tray in a medium-hot oven to keep warm until all the batches are cooked.

Thai Vermicelli Soup

 SERVES 4

 PREP TIME:
10 minutes
plus soaking

 COOKING TIME:
15 minutes

nutritional information
per serving — 177 kcals, 5.5g fat, 0.4g sat fat, 2g total sugars, 0.9g salt

Try this light, spicy soup at the beginning of a Thai inspired meal - it will awaken the taste buds. Shiitake mushrooms really give an authentic flavour and are available in larger supermarkets or Asian stores.

INGREDIENTS

15 g/½ oz dried shiitake mushrooms
1.2 litres/2 pints vegetable stock
1 tbsp groundnut oil
4 spring onions, sliced
115 g/4 oz baby corn, sliced
2 garlic cloves, crushed
2 fresh kaffir lime leaves, chopped
2 tbsp red curry paste
85 g/3 oz rice vermicelli noodles
1 tbsp light soy sauce
2 tbsp chopped fresh coriander, to garnish

1. Place the mushrooms in a bowl, cover with the vegetable stock and leave to soak for 20 minutes.

2. Heat the groundnut oil in a saucepan over a medium heat. Add the spring onions, baby corn, garlic and kaffir lime leaves. Fry for 3 minutes to soften.

3. Add the red curry paste, soaked mushrooms and their soaking liquid. Bring to the boil and simmer for 5 minutes, stirring occasionally.

4. Add the noodles and soy sauce to the red curry mixture in the pan. Return the pan to the boil and simmer for a further 4 minutes until the noodles are just cooked. Ladle into warmed bowls, garnish with the chopped coriander and serve immediately.

1

2

3

SOMETHING DIFFERENT
Use corncobs instead
of baby corn. Stand
the cobs upright on
a board and with a
sharp knife cut down
from the top to remove
all the kernels from
one or two cobs.

Grilled Halloumi Kebabs on Fennel & White Bean Salad

 SERVES 4

 PREP TIME:
10 minutes

 COOKING TIME:
8–10 minutes

nutritional information
per serving — 338 kcals, 24g fat, 10g sat fat, 2.5g total sugars, 1.2g salt

Made from sheep's milk, halloumi is the perfect choice for mini kebabs as it keeps its shape when grilled.

INGREDIENTS

200 g/7 oz vegetarian halloumi cheese
1 garlic clove, crushed
1 fennel bulb, thinly sliced
1 small red onion, thinly sliced
400 g/14 oz canned cannellini beans, drained
1–2 tbsp balsamic vinegar, to serve

dressing
finely grated rind and juice of 1 lemon
3 tbsp chopped fresh flat-leaf parsley
4 tbsp olive oil
salt and pepper

1. For the dressing, mix together the lemon rind and juice, parsley and oil with salt and pepper to taste.

2. Cut the halloumi into 2-cm/¾-inch cubes, thread onto four pre-soaked wooden skewers and brush with half the dressing.

3. Preheat the grill to high. Cook the skewers under the preheated grill for 6–8 minutes, turning once, until golden.

4. Heat the remaining dressing and the garlic in a small pan until boiling. Combine with the fennel, onion and beans.

5. Serve the skewers with the salad, sprinkled with a little balsamic vinegar.

2

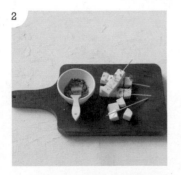

3

4

SOMETHING DIFFERENT
If fennel is not in season, replace with thinly sliced celery sticks and use the leafy tops as garnish.

Avocado Salad with Lime Dressing *38*

Eggs Florentine *40*

Crunchy Thai-style Salad *42*

Couscous with Roast Cherry Tomatoes & Pine Nuts *44*

Courgette Fritters with Eggs & Caramelized Onions *46*

Caramelized Apple & Blue Cheese Salad *48*

Melting Mozzarella Bagels *50*

Aubergine, Pepper & Basil Crêpe Rolls *52*

Glazed Beetroot & Egg Sourdough Toasties *54*

Creamy Mushroom Pancakes *56*

Thai Tofu Cakes with Chilli Dip *58*

Greek Salad Crostini *60*

Spicy Polenta with Poached Eggs *62*

Couscous Salad with Roasted Butternut Squash *64*

Salads & Light Meals

Avocado Salad with Lime Dressing

 SERVES 4

 PREP TIME: 10 minutes

 COOKING TIME: No cooking

nutritional information per serving	290 kcals, 28g fat, 5g sat fat, 4.5g total sugars, 0.1g salt

A perfect choice for a light lunch, this salad is as delightful to look at as it is to eat.

INGREDIENTS

60 g/2¼ oz mixed red and green lettuce leaves

60 g/2¼ oz wild rocket

4 spring onions, finely diced

5 tomatoes, sliced

25 g/1 oz walnuts, toasted and chopped

2 avocados

1 tbsp lemon juice

lime dressing

1 tbsp lime juice

1 tsp French mustard

1 tbsp sour cream

1 tbsp chopped fresh parsley or coriander

3 tbsp extra virgin olive oil

pinch of sugar

salt and pepper

1. Wash and drain the lettuce and rocket, if necessary. Shred all the leaves and arrange in the bottom of a large salad bowl. Add the spring onions, tomatoes and walnuts.

2. Stone, peel and thinly slice or dice the avocados. Brush with the lemon juice to prevent discoloration, then transfer to the salad bowl. Gently mix together.

3. To make the dressing, put all the dressing ingredients in a screw-top jar and shake well. Drizzle over the salad and serve immediately.

2

3

Eggs Florentine

 SERVES 4   PREP TIME: 20 minutes   COOKING TIME: 35–40 minutes

nutritional information per serving	477 kcals, 39g fat, 16g sat fat, 7g total sugars, 1.1g salt

This classic dish is always a favourite for a special breakfast or a lazy weekend brunch.

INGREDIENTS

450 g/1 lb fresh spinach leaves, thoroughly washed

55 g/2 oz unsalted butter, plus extra for greasing

55 g/2 oz button mushrooms, sliced

55 g/2 oz pine nuts, toasted

6 spring onions, chopped

4 eggs

25 g/1 oz plain wholemeal flour

300 ml/10 fl oz milk, warmed

1 tsp prepared English mustard

85 g/3 oz mature vegetarian Cheddar cheese, grated

salt and pepper

1. Preheat the oven to 190°C/375°F/Gas Mark 5. Shake off any excess water from the spinach, put into a large saucepan over a medium heat with only the water clinging to the leaves and sprinkle with a little salt. Cover and cook for 2–3 minutes, or until wilted. Drain, pressing out any excess liquid, then chop and place in a greased ovenproof dish.

2. Heat 15 g/½ oz of the butter in a small saucepan over a medium heat, add the mushrooms and cook for 2 minutes, stirring frequently. Add the pine nuts and spring onions and cook for a further 2 minutes. Remove from the heat, season to taste with salt and pepper and scatter over the spinach. Reserve and keep warm.

3. Meanwhile, fill a frying pan with cold water and bring to the boil, then reduce the heat to a gentle simmer. Carefully break an egg into a cup and slip it into the water. Add the remaining eggs and cook for 4–5 minutes, or until set. Carefully remove with a slotted spoon and arrange on top of the spinach mixture.

4. Melt the remaining butter in a saucepan and stir in the flour. Cook for 2 minutes, then remove from the heat and gradually stir in the milk. Return to the heat and cook, stirring constantly, until the mixture comes to the boil and has thickened. Stir in the mustard, then 55 g/ 2 oz of the cheese. Continue stirring until the cheese has melted. Add salt and pepper to taste, then pour over the eggs, completely covering them. Sprinkle with the remaining cheese.

5. Cook in the preheated oven for 20–25 minutes, or until piping hot and the top is golden brown and bubbling. Serve immediately.

Crunchy Thai-style Salad

 SERVES 4   PREP TIME: 10 minutes   COOKING TIME: No cooking

nutritional information per serving	74 kcals, 3g fat, 0.5g sat fat, 8g total sugars, 1.4g salt

Crispy, crunchy and full of flavour, this salad uses fragrant firm mangoes.

INGREDIENTS

1 slightly under ripe mango

5 Romaine or Cos lettuce leaves, torn into pieces

100 g/3½ oz beansprouts

handful of fresh coriander leaves

25 g/1 oz roasted unsalted peanuts, crushed

dressing
juice of 1 lime

2 tbsp light soy sauce

1 tsp soft light brown sugar

1 shallot, very thinly sliced

1 garlic clove, finely chopped

1 red bird's eye chilli, very thinly sliced

1 tbsp chopped fresh mint

1. To make the dressing, mix the lime juice, soy sauce and sugar together in a bowl then stir in the shallot, garlic, chilli and mint.

2. Peel the mango using a sharp knife or potato peeler. Slice the flesh from either side and around the stone. Thinly slice or shred the flesh.

3. Place the torn lettuce, beansprouts, coriander leaves and mango in a serving bowl. Gently toss together. Spoon the dressing over the top, scatter with the peanuts and serve immediately.

Couscous with Roast Cherry Tomatoes & Pine Nuts

 SERVES 4

 PREP TIME:
10 minutes
plus standing

 COOKING TIME:
8 minutes

nutritional information
per serving · 210 kcals, 14g fat, 1.5g sat fat, 2.5g total sugars, trace salt

This looks really pretty made with mixed red and yellow cherry tomatoes.

INGREDIENTS

300 g/10½ oz cherry tomatoes
3 tbsp olive oil
125 g/4½ oz couscous
200 ml/7 fl oz boiling water
30 g/1 oz pine nuts, toasted
5 tbsp roughly chopped fresh mint
finely grated zest of 1 lemon
½ tbsp lemon juice
salt and pepper

1. Preheat the oven to 220°C/425°F/Gas Mark 7. Place the tomatoes and 1 tablespoon of the oil in an ovenproof dish. Toss together, then roast for 7–8 minutes in the preheated oven until the tomatoes are soft and the skins have burst. Leave to stand for 5 minutes.

2. Put the couscous in a heatproof bowl. Pour over the boiling water, cover and leave to stand for 8–10 minutes until soft and the liquid is absorbed. Fluff up with a fork.

3. Add the tomatoes and their juices, the pine nuts, mint, lemon zest, lemon juice and the remaining oil to the couscous. Season with salt and pepper, then gently toss together. Serve warm or cold.

1

1

2

GOES WELL WITH
This goes well with a crisp green salad and some vegetarian feta cheese or chargrilled halloumi.

Courgette Fritters with Eggs & Caramelized Onions

 SERVES 4

 PREP TIME:
20 minutes
plus cooling

 COOKING TIME:
45 minutes

nutritional information per serving	572 kcals, 33g fat, 6g sat fat, 14g total sugars, 0.8g salt

Make the caramelized onions in advance and store in the refrigerator for up to a week. If the batter mixture for the fritters seems too thick, stir in a little extra milk.

INGREDIENTS

2 tbsp extra virgin olive oil

5 red onions, sliced

1 tbsp soft brown sugar

200 g/7 oz self-raising flour

1 egg, lightly beaten, plus 4 eggs for poaching or frying

200 ml/7 fl oz milk

2 courgettes, grated

225 ml/8 fl oz sunflower oil

salt and pepper

1. Heat the olive oil in a large heavy-based saucepan over a medium heat, add the onions and cook for 5 minutes, or until softened. Stir in the sugar and reduce the heat, cover and cook for 30 minutes, or until the onions are deep brown in colour, stirring occasionally. Season to taste with salt and pepper and leave to cool.

2. To make the fritters, place the flour in a large bowl and make a well in the centre. Whisk the beaten egg and milk together and incorporate into the flour, using a wooden spoon to make a batter. Season to taste with salt and pepper and stir in the grated courgettes.

3. Heat the sunflower oil in a wide deep-sided pan and drop in tablespoons of the batter. Cook until golden brown on both sides, turning once. Drain on kitchen paper and keep warm.

4. Poach or fry the eggs, as you prefer. To serve, place three fritters on each individual plate, place an egg on top and spoon over some of the caramelized onions. Serve immediately.

Caramelized Apple & Blue Cheese Salad

 SERVES 2   PREP TIME: 10 minutes, plus cooling   COOKING TIME: 5 minutes

nutritional information per serving   410 kcals, 33g fat, 11g sat fat, 19g total sugars, 0.7g salt

Apples caramelize better if there are fewer in the pan, so if you want to make more, cook in batches.

INGREDIENTS

15 g/½ oz butter

2 tbsp sunflower oil or rapeseed oil

1 large red-skinned dessert apple, such as Pink Lady, cored and cut into thin wedges

2 tsp clear honey

1½ tsp fresh thyme leaves

1½ tbsp white wine vinegar

2 tsp wholegrain mustard

55 g/2 oz mixed salad leaves

40 g/1½ oz vegetarian blue cheese, crumbled

25 g/1 oz walnuts, toasted and roughly chopped

2 tbsp snipped chives

salt and pepper

1. Heat the butter with 1 teaspoon of the oil in a frying pan. Add the apples and fry for 2 minutes, stirring occasionally, until soft. Add the honey and thyme and continue to cook until the apples begin to caramelize. Remove from the heat.

2. Stir in the remaining oil, the vinegar and mustard. Season with pepper and a little salt and leave to cool slightly.

3. Place the salad leaves, cheese, walnuts and chives in a serving bowl. Spoon over the apples and warm dressing from the pan. Toss together and serve immediately.

1

2

3

SOMETHING DIFFERENT
You could use firm ripe pears instead of apples, and toasted pine nuts instead of walnuts.

Melting Mozzarella Bagels

 SERVES 4   PREP TIME: 10 minutes   COOKING TIME: 20 minutes

nutritional information per serving	419 kcals, 19g fat, 7g sat fat, 7g total sugars, 1.5g salt

A really filling start to the day, the quantities can easily be increased to feed a larger crowd. Swap the basil leaves for rocket if you prefer.

INGREDIENTS

½ aubergine, thinly sliced

3–4 tbsp olive oil

4 onion bagels or plain bagels

175 g/6 oz vegetarian mozzarella cheese, sliced

1 beef tomato, thinly sliced

salt and pepper

6–8 fresh basil leaves, torn in half if large, to serve

1. Preheat a griddle pan until smoking. Brush the aubergine slices with a little of the oil, place on the pan and cook for 2 minutes on each side until tender and lightly charred.

2. Preheat the oven to 190°C/375°F/Gas Mark 5. Split the bagels in half and drizzle the cut sides with the remaining oil. Divide the cheese slices between the bagel bases and arrange the slices of tomato and aubergine on top. Season with salt and pepper and replace the bagel tops.

3. Place on a baking tray and bake in the preheated oven for 15 minutes until the cheese has melted and the bagels are beginning to toast around the edges. Add a few fresh basil leaves to each bagel and serve immediately.

1

2

3

BE PREPARED
Get ahead by
assembling the
bagels and
placing them in
the refrigerator
the night before,
ready to pop in
the oven at the
last minute.

Aubergine, Pepper & Basil Crêpe Rolls

 SERVES 4

 PREP TIME:
15 minutes
plus standing

 COOKING TIME:
15 minutes

nutritional information per serving	560 kcals, 41g fat, 22g sat fat, 9g total sugars, 0.6g salt

Serve these vegetable and cheese rolls wrapped in paper napkins for fast food at home.

INGREDIENTS

150 g/5½ oz plain white flour
pinch of salt
250 ml/9 fl oz milk
100 ml/3½ fl oz water
1 large egg
2 tbsp olive oil
sunflower oil, for greasing

filling
2 large aubergines
olive oil, for brushing
2 large red peppers, halved and deseeded
250 g/9 oz vegetarian soft cream cheese
handful of fresh basil leaves
salt and pepper

1. For the filling, slice the aubergines lengthwise into 8-mm/⅜-inch thick slices, sprinkle with salt and leave to drain for about 20 minutes. Rinse and dry.

2. Preheat the grill to high. Arrange the aubergine slices on a baking sheet in a single layer, brush with olive oil and grill until golden, turning once. Arrange the red peppers, cut side down, on a baking sheet in a single layer and grill until blackened. Remove the skins and slice.

3. Sift the flour and salt into a bowl. Add the milk, water, egg and oil and whisk to a smooth, bubbly batter. Leave to stand for 15 minutes.

4. Lightly grease a 20-cm/8-inch frying pan and heat over a medium heat. Pour in enough batter to just cover the pan, swirling to cover in a thin, even layer. Cook until the underside is golden, then flip or turn with a palette knife and cook the other side until golden brown.

5. Repeat this process using the remaining batter. Interleave the cooked crêpes with kitchen paper and keep warm.

6. Arrange the pancakes in pairs, slightly overlapping. Spread with cheese and top with the aubergines, red peppers, basil and salt and pepper to taste. Roll up firmly from one short side. Cut in half diagonally and serve immediately.

Glazed Beetroot & Egg Sourdough Toasties

 SERVES 4   PREP TIME: 10 minutes   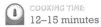 COOKING TIME: 12–15 minutes

nutritional information per serving	404 kcals, 24g fat, 4g sat fat, 14g total sugars, 1.4g salt

Try this traditional combination of ruby red beetroot and chopped egg served on sourdough bread for a great lunch dish.

INGREDIENTS

4 eggs

500 g/1 lb 2 oz cooked beetroot (fresh or vacuum-packed without vinegar)

2 tsp sugar

5 tsp cider vinegar

4 slices sourdough bread (from a long oval loaf)

6 tbsp olive oil

1 tbsp Dijon mustard

3 tbsp chopped fresh dill, plus extra sprigs to garnish

salt and pepper

1. Boil the eggs for 8 minutes, then drain, shell and chop them. Set aside. Dice the beetroot quite small and place in a small bowl. Mix in half the sugar, 1 tsp of the cider vinegar and seasoning.

2. Preheat the grill to a medium–high setting. Brush the bread with a little olive oil and toast on one side on the rack in the grill pan for 2–3 minutes, until crisp and golden.

3. Meanwhile, trickle 1 tsp of the remaining oil over the beetroot. Whisk the remaining cider vinegar, mustard and remaining sugar together with seasoning. Gradually whisk in the remaining oil to make a thick dressing. Stir in the dill and taste for seasoning – it should be sweet and mustardy, with a sharpness – add more sugar or vinegar if you wish.

4. Turn the bread and top with the beetroot, giving it a stir first, covering the slices right up to the crusts. Glaze the beetroot under the grill for 2–3 minutes, until browned in places.

5. Cut the slices in half or quarters and top with egg. Drizzle with a little dressing, garnish with the dill sprigs and serve immediately.

Creamy Mushroom Pancakes

 SERVES 2   PREP TIME: 10 minutes   COOKING TIME: 5 minutes

nutritional information per serving	562 kcals, 39g fat, 15g sat fat, 8g total sugars, 0.6g salt

This really quick mushroom filling makes a perfect partner for wholemeal pancakes.

INGREDIENTS

50 ml/2 fl oz light olive oil

250 g/9 oz chestnut mushrooms, sliced

1 tsp dried thyme or 2 tsp fresh thyme leaves

2 tbsp chopped fresh flat-leaf parsley

200 ml/7 fl oz half-fat crème fraîche

80 g/2¾ oz wholemeal self-raising flour

1 egg

200 ml/7 fl oz semi-skimmed milk

salt and pepper

1. Heat 2 tablespoons of the oil in a frying pan. Add the mushrooms, thyme and half of the parsley. Season to taste with salt and pepper and cook over a high heat for 2 minutes. Stir in the crème fraîche.

2. Beat together the flour, egg and milk in a bowl and season to taste with salt and pepper. Heat ½ teaspoon of the remaining oil in a 20-cm/8-inch non-stick frying pan until very hot. Add a quarter of the batter, tilting the pan to cover the base. Cook over a high heat for 30 seconds, then flip the pancake and cook for a further minute. Slide it onto a warmed plate. Repeat to make three more pancakes.

3. Spoon a quarter of the mushroom mixture into the centre of each pancake and fold over. Sprinkle with the remaining parsley and serve.

1

2

3

BE PREPARED
Make and fill
the pancakes
in advance and
arrange in an
ovenproof dish.
Cover with foil
and reheat in a
medium-hot oven
until the filling
is bubbling.

Thai Tofu Cakes with Chilli Dip

 SERVES 4

 PREP TIME:
10 minutes
plus chilling

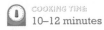 COOKING TIME:
10–12 minutes

nutritional information per serving	226 kcals, 10g fat, 1.5g sat fat, 5g total sugars, 0.7g salt

Similar to a fish cake, this Thai favourite would also make a great starter or snack with drinks.

INGREDIENTS

300 g/10½ oz firm tofu, drained weight, coarsely grated

1 lemon grass stalk, finely chopped

2 garlic cloves, chopped

2.5-cm/1-inch piece fresh ginger, grated

2 kaffir lime leaves, finely chopped (optional)

2 shallots, finely chopped

2 fresh red chillies, deseeded and finely chopped

4 tbsp chopped fresh coriander

90 g/3¼ oz plain flour, plus extra for dusting

½ tsp salt

corn oil, for cooking

chilli dip

3 tbsp white distilled vinegar

2 spring onions, finely sliced

1 tbsp caster sugar

2 fresh chillies, chopped

2 tbsp chopped fresh coriander

pinch of salt

1. To make the chilli dip, mix all the ingredients together in a small serving bowl and set aside.

2. Mix the tofu with the lemon grass, garlic, ginger, lime leaves, if using, shallots, chillies and coriander in a mixing bowl. Stir in the flour and salt to make a coarse, sticky paste. Cover and chill in the refrigerator for 1 hour to let the mixture firm up slightly.

3. Form the mixture into eight large walnut-sized balls and, using floured hands, flatten into circles. Heat enough oil to cover the bottom of a large, heavy-based frying pan over medium heat. Cook the cakes in two batches, turning halfway through, for 4–6 minutes, or until golden brown. Drain on kitchen paper and serve warm with the chilli dip.

Greek Salad Crostini

 SERVES 2

 PREP TIME:
10 minutes

 COOKING TIME:
5 minutes

nutritional information per serving	655 kcals, 50g fat, 18g sat fat, 11g total sugars, 4.4g salt

Crisp toasted country bread topped with a salad that packs in the flavours.

INGREDIENTS

1 garlic clove, crushed

4 tbsp olive oil

2 thick slices from a large, seeded loaf

200 g/7 oz vegetarian feta cheese, diced

pepper

¼ cucumber, finely diced

25 g/1 oz black olives, sliced

4 plum tomatoes, diced

½ small onion, chopped

2 sprigs fresh mint leaves, shredded

2 sprigs fresh oregano leaves, chopped

¼ tsp sugar

1 heart Little Gem lettuce, finely shredded

½ tsp toasted sesame seeds

2 tsp pine nuts (optional)

1. Preheat the grill to a medium–high setting. Mix the garlic and olive oil in a bowl large enough to mix all the salad ingredients.

2. Place the bread on the rack in the grill pan. Brush lightly with the garlic oil and toast well away from the heat for 2–3 minutes, until crisp and golden. Turn the bread and brush lightly with more oil, then toast again.

3. Add the feta cheese to the garlic oil remaining in the bowl and season with pepper (the cheese and olives usually provide enough salt). Mix in the cucumber, olives, tomatoes, onion, mint and oregano. Sprinkle with the sugar and mix well. Finally, lightly mix in the lettuce.

4. Transfer the crostini to plates and spoon the salad and its juices over them. Sprinkle with the sesame seeds and pine nuts (if using) and serve immediately, while the crostini are hot and crisp.

3

3

Spicy Polenta with Poached Eggs

 SERVES 4   PREP TIME: 10 minutes plus cooling    COOKING TIME: 11–15 minutes

nutritional information per serving	414 kcals, 24g fat, 11g sat fat, 1g total sugars, 1g salt

To use the polenta trimmings, chop roughly, place in a shallow ovenproof dish, brush with melted butter and grill for 3 minutes. Serve as an unusual side dish.

INGREDIENTS

oil, for oiling

600 ml/1 pint water

150 g/5½ oz quick-cook polenta

85 g/3 oz freshly grated vegetarian Parmesan-style cheese

40 g/1½ oz butter

½–1 red chilli, deseeded and very finely chopped

200 g/7 oz baby spinach leaves, or a mixture of baby spinach leaves and rocket leaves

2 tsp white wine vinegar

4 large eggs

salt and pepper

1. Lightly oil an 18-cm/7-inch square cake tin. Bring the water to the boil in a saucepan. Add the polenta in a thin stream and cook, stirring, over a medium–low heat for 3 minutes until thick. Stir in 55 g/2 oz of the cheese, 30 g/1 oz of the butter and the chilli. Working quickly, transfer to the prepared tin and level the surface. Set aside for 30 minutes until cool and firm, then cut out four rounds with a 9-cm/3½-inch cutter and transfer to a baking tray.

2. Wash the spinach and place in a large saucepan with the water clinging to the leaves. Cover and cook for 2–3 minutes until wilted, then squeeze out the excess water between two plates. Return to the pan.

3. Preheat the grill to high. Sprinkle the polenta rounds with the remaining cheese, place under the preheated grill and cook for 3 minutes until brown and bubbling on the top. Keep warm. Meanwhile, add the remaining butter and salt and pepper to taste to the spinach and heat through.

4. Half fill a saucepan with water, add the vinegar and bring to simmering point. Crack the eggs into cups and slide gently into the water. Cook over a low heat, without allowing the water to boil, for 3 minutes until the whites are firm and the yolk is still soft. Scoop out with a slotted spoon and drain briefly on kitchen paper.

5. To serve, place the polenta rounds on four warmed plates and divide the spinach between them. Top with the eggs and sprinkle with a little salt and pepper. Serve immediately.

Couscous Salad with Roasted Butternut Squash

 SERVES 4 PREP TIME: 10 minutes  COOKING TIME: 30–40 minutes

nutritional information per serving	370 kcals, 13g fat, 2g sat fat, 19g total sugars, trace salt

Couscous is eaten around the Mediterranean and can be cooked in many ways, including this Moroccan-inspired salad.

INGREDIENTS

2 tbsp honey

4 tbsp olive oil

1 butternut squash, peeled, deseeded and cut into 2-cm/¾-inch chunks

250 g/9 oz couscous

400 ml/14 fl oz low-salt vegetable stock

½ cucumber, diced

1 courgette, diced

1 red pepper, deseeded and diced

juice of ½ lemon

2 tbsp chopped fresh parsley

salt and pepper

1. Preheat the oven to 190°C/375°F/Gas Mark 5. Mix half the honey with 1 tablespoon of the oil in a large bowl, add the squash and toss well to coat. Tip into a roasting tin and roast in the preheated oven for 30–40 minutes until soft and golden.

2. Meanwhile, put the couscous in a heatproof bowl. Heat the stock in a saucepan and pour over the couscous, cover and leave for 3 minutes. Add 1 tablespoon of the remaining oil and fork through, then stir in the diced cucumber, courgette and red pepper. Re-cover and keep warm.

3. Whisk the remaining honey and oil with the lemon juice in a jug and season to taste with salt and pepper. Stir the mixture through the couscous.

4. To serve, top the couscous with the roasted squash and sprinkle with the parsley.

1

2

2

BE PREPARED
This dish can
also be made
in advance and
served cold.
Great for a
picnic.

Lentil Bolognese *68*

Smoky Mushroom & Coriander Burgers *70*

Leek, Herb & Mushroom Risotto *72*

Stir-fried Rice with Green Vegetables *74*

Pasta with Two Cheeses & Walnuts *76*

Mediterranean Vegetables with Feta & Olives *78*

Teriyaki Tofu Stir-fry *80*

Rigatoni with Roast Courgette, Tomato & Mascarpone Sauce *82*

Griddled Courgette & Feta Pizza *84*

New Potato, Feta & Herb Frittata *86*

Bean & Vegetable Chilli *88*

Quinoa with Roasted Vegetables *90*

Lattice Flan *92*

Mixed Nut Roast with Cranberry & Red Wine Sauce *94*

Main Meals

Lentil Bolognese

 SERVES 4

 PREP TIME:
15 minutes

 COOKING TIME:
45–55 minutes

nutritional information per serving	500 kcals, 8g fat, 1g sat fat, 16.5g total sugars, 0.3g salt

No vegetarian kitchen should be without a recipe for this popular pasta sauce.

INGREDIENTS

175 g/6 oz green lentils

2 tbsp olive oil

1 large onion, chopped

2 garlic cloves, crushed

2 carrots, chopped

2 celery sticks, chopped

800 g/1 lb 12 oz canned chopped tomatoes

150 ml/5 fl oz vegetable stock

1 red pepper, deseeded and chopped

2 tbsp tomato purée

2 tsp very finely chopped fresh rosemary

1 tsp dried oregano

280 g/10 oz dried spaghetti or linguine

handful of basil leaves, torn

salt and pepper

freshly grated vegetarian Parmesan-style cheese, to serve

1. Put the lentils in a saucepan and cover with cold water. Bring to the boil and simmer for 20–30 minutes until just tender. Drain well.

2. Meanwhile, heat the oil in a large saucepan. Add the onion, garlic, carrots and celery. Cover and cook over a low heat for 5 minutes. Stir in the tomatoes, stock, red pepper, tomato purée, rosemary and oregano. Cover and simmer for 20 minutes until the sauce is thickened and the vegetables are tender. Add the lentils and cook, stirring, for a further 5 minutes. Season with salt and pepper.

3. While the sauce is cooking, bring a large saucepan of lightly salted water to the boil. Add the spaghetti, bring back to the boil and cook for 10 minutes, or until tender but still firm to the bite. Drain well, then divide the spaghetti between four warmed bowls. Spoon the sauce over the top and scatter with the basil leaves. Serve immediately with the grated cheese.

Smoky Mushroom & Coriander Burgers

 SERVES 6   PREP TIME: 15 minutes    COOKING TIME: 10–15 minutes

nutritional information **per serving**   170 kcals, 6g fat, 0.8g sat fat, 5g total sugars, 1.8g salt

Children will love helping mix and shape these vegan burgers.

INGREDIENTS

425 g/15 oz canned red kidney beans, rinsed and drained

2 tbsp sunflower oil or vegetable oil, plus extra for brushing

1 onion, finely chopped

115 g/4 oz mushrooms, finely chopped

1 large carrot, coarsely grated

2 tsp smoked paprika

70 g/2½ oz porridge oats

3 tbsp dark soy sauce

2 tbsp tomato purée

30 g/1 oz fresh coriander, including stalks, chopped

3 tbsp plain flour

salt and pepper

to serve
soft rolls

salad leaves

sliced avocado

tomato salsa or relish

1. Place the beans in a large bowl and mash as thoroughly as you can with a potato masher. Heat the oil in a frying pan, add the onion and fry for 2 minutes until translucent. Add the mushrooms, carrot and paprika and fry for a further 4 minutes until the vegetables are soft.

2. Add the fried vegetables to the beans with the oats, soy sauce, tomato purée and coriander. Season with salt and pepper and mix well. Divide into six equal portions and shape into burgers, then turn in the flour to coat lightly.

3. Preheat a griddle pan until smoking. Lightly brush the tops of the burgers with oil, then place oiled side down on the pan. Cook over a medium heat for 2–3 minutes until lightly charred underneath. Lightly brush the tops with oil, turn and cook for a further 2-3 minutes on the other side. Serve hot in soft rolls with salad leaves, avocado slices and salsa.

Leek, Herb & Mushroom Risotto

 SERVES 8   PREP TIME: 15 minutes   COOKING TIME: 30–35 minutes

nutritional information per serving	243 kcals, 8.5g fat, 4g sat fat, 0.5g total sugars, 0.2g salt

A filling and comforting dish. Use a mixture of cultivated and wild mushrooms rather than chestnut mushrooms, if you prefer.

INGREDIENTS

1 litre/1¾ pints hot vegetable stock
2 tbsp olive oil
1 small leek, roughly chopped
3 garlic cloves, crushed
1 tbsp fresh thyme
250 g/9 oz chestnut mushrooms, sliced
300 g/10½ oz arborio rice
175 ml/6 fl oz dry white wine
30 g/1 oz butter
55 g/2 oz freshly grated vegetarian Parmesan-style cheese
2 tbsp snipped fresh chives, plus extra to serve
salt and pepper
rocket leaves and vegetarian Parmesan-style cheese shavings, to garnish

1. Keep the stock hot in a saucepan set over a medium heat. Heat the oil in a separate saucepan over a low heat. Add the leek, garlic and thyme and cook for 5 minutes until soft. Add the mushrooms and continue to cook for a further 4 minutes until soft.

2. Stir in the rice and cook stirring for 1 minute, then add the wine and heat rapidly until the liquid has almost completely evaporated.

3. Add a ladleful of stock and cook over a medium heat, stirring, until it is absorbed by the rice. Continue adding the stock in the same way until it is all used up and the rice is creamy, plump and tender.

4. If the risotto is a little undercooked add a splash of water and continue cooking until creamy. Adding extra stock may make the risotto too salty.

5. Stir in the butter, followed by the cheese and chives. Season with salt and pepper. Serve in warmed bowls topped with rocket leaves, chives and cheese shavings.

Stir-fried Rice with Green Vegetables

 SERVES 4　　 PREP TIME:
5 minutes
plus cooling　　 COOKING TIME:
20–25 minutes

nutritional information per serving	288 kcals, 7g fat, 0.8g sat fat, 3g total sugars, 0.2g salt

Thai basil should not be confused with sweet basil used in many Italian dishes. Thai basil has a slight liquorice flavour which complements this dish perfectly.

INGREDIENTS

225 g/8 oz jasmine rice
2 tbsp vegetable or peanut oil
1 tbsp green curry paste
6 spring onions, sliced
2 garlic cloves, crushed
1 courgette, cut into thin sticks
115 g/4 oz French beans
175 g/6 oz asparagus, trimmed
3–4 fresh Thai basil leaves

1. Cook the rice in lightly salted boiling water for 12–15 minutes, drain well, cover, cool thoroughly and chill.

2. Heat the oil in a wok and stir-fry the curry paste for 1 minute. Add the spring onions and garlic and stir-fry for 1 minute.

3. Add the courgette, beans and asparagus and stir-fry for 3–4 minutes, until just tender. Break up the rice and add it to the wok. Cook, stirring constantly for 2–3 minutes, until the rice is hot. Stir in the basil and serve immediately.

1

2

3

FREEZING TIP
Thai basil can be frozen in small quantities. Chop the leaves in a food processor adding a little vegetable oil to coat. Pack into ice cube trays and freeze.

Pasta with Two Cheeses & Walnuts

 SERVES 4

 PREP TIME:
5 minutes

 COOKING TIME:
15 minutes

nutritional information per serving	838 kcals, 49g fat, 20g sat fat, 5g total sugars, 0.9g salt

The perfect dish to eat curled up on the sofa watching TV. Alternatively, it makes a brilliant supper dish in a more formal setting served with a crisp salad and a glass of wine.

INGREDIENTS

350 g/12 oz dried penne

280 g/10 oz fresh or frozen peas

150 g/5½ oz vegetarian soft cheese with garlic and herbs

175 g/6 oz baby spinach leaves

100 g/3½ oz vegetarian blue cheese, cut into small cubes

115 g/4 oz walnuts, roughly chopped

salt and pepper

1. Cook the pasta in a large saucepan of lightly salted boiling water for 8–10 minutes, adding the peas for the final 2 minutes. Drain, reserving 125 ml/4 fl oz of the hot cooking liquid.

2. Return the pan to the heat. Add the reserved cooking liquid and the soft cheese. Heat, stirring, until melted and smooth.

3. Remove from the heat, then add the spinach to the pan followed by the pasta, peas, blue cheese and walnuts. Season to taste with pepper and toss together, until the spinach has wilted and the cheese has started to melt. Serve immediately.

1

2

3

COOK'S NOTE
A splash of olive oil added to the cooking water helps prevent the pasta sticking together.

Mediterranean Vegetables with Feta & Olives

 SERVES 4

 PREP TIME: 10 minutes

 COOKING TIME: 20–25 minutes

nutritional information per serving	240 kcals, 12g fat, 2.5g sat fat, 11g total sugars, 0.7g salt

Let the wonderful aromas wafting from the kitchen remind you of warm evenings dining alfresco.

INGREDIENTS

1 red onion, sliced into thick rings

1 small aubergine, thickly sliced

2 large mushrooms, halved

3 red peppers, halved and deseeded

3 plum tomatoes, peeled and diced

2 garlic cloves, very finely chopped

1 tbsp chopped fresh flat-leaf parsley

1 tsp chopped fresh rosemary

1 tsp dried thyme or oregano

finely grated rind of 1 lemon

75 g/2¾ oz stale, coarse breadcrumbs

3 tbsp olive oil, plus extra for brushing

6–8 black olives, stoned and sliced

25 g/1 oz vegetarian feta cheese (drained weight), cut into 1-cm/½-inch cubes

salt and pepper

1. Preheat the grill to medium. Put the onion, aubergine, mushrooms and peppers on a large baking tray, placing the peppers cut-side down. Brush with a little oil. Cook under the preheated grill for 10–12 minutes, turning the onion, aubergine and mushrooms halfway through, until beginning to blacken. Cut into even-sized chunks.

2. Preheat the oven to 220°C/425°F/Gas Mark 7. Place the grilled vegetables in a shallow ovenproof dish and arrange the tomatoes on top. Season to taste with salt and pepper.

3. In a bowl, combine the garlic, parsley, rosemary, thyme and lemon rind with the breadcrumbs. Season to taste with pepper. Add the oil to bind the mixture together. Scatter the breadcrumb mixture over the vegetables, followed by the olives and feta cheese.

4. Bake in the preheated oven for 10–15 minutes, or until the vegetables are heated through and the topping is crisp. Serve immediately.

Teriyaki Tofu Stir-fry

 SERVES 2   PREP TIME: 15 minutes   COOKING TIME: 15 minutes

nutritional information
per serving   738 kcals, 25g fat, 4g sat fat, 33g total sugars, 4.6g salt

*Try this method of dry-frying tofu which firms up
the texture without adding extra calories and fat.*

INGREDIENTS

140 g/5 oz medium egg noodles
200 g/7 oz firm tofu, drained
2 tbsp sunflower oil or vegetable oil
1 red pepper, deseeded and thinly sliced
140 g/5 oz baby corn, diagonally sliced
200 g/7 oz choi sum, cut into 4-cm/1½-inch pieces
salt

sauce
3 tbsp tamari or dark soy sauce
3 tbsp rice wine
3 tbsp clear honey
1 tbsp cornflour
1 tbsp finely grated fresh ginger
1–2 garlic cloves, crushed
250 ml/9 fl oz water

1. Bring a large saucepan of lightly salted water to the boil. Add the noodles, bring back to the boil and cook for 4 minutes, or until tender but still firm to the bite. Drain.

2. Meanwhile, cut the tofu into 15-mm/⅝-inch slices and then into bite-sized pieces. Pat dry on plenty of kitchen paper. Heat a non-stick or well-seasoned frying pan over a medium–low heat, then add the tofu and cook for 3 minutes, without moving the pieces around the pan, until golden brown underneath. Turn and cook for a further 2–3 minutes on the other side. Transfer to a plate.

3. To make the sauce, mix the tamari, rice wine, honey, cornflour, ginger and garlic together in a jug until well blended, then stir in the water. Set aside.

4. Heat the oil in a wok or a large, heavy-based frying pan. Add the pepper and baby corn, and stir-fry for 3 minutes. Add the choi sum and stir-fry for a further 2 minutes. Pour in the sauce and heat, stirring constantly, until it boils and thickens. Add the noodles and tofu and toss together over the heat for a further 1–2 minutes until heated through. Serve immediately.

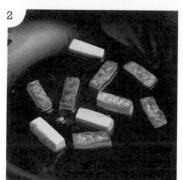

Rigatoni with Roast Courgette, Tomato & Mascarpone Sauce

 SERVES 4   PREP TIME: 15 minutes   COOKING TIME: 30–35 minutes

nutritional information per serving	520 kcals, 24g fat, 10g sat fat, 11g total sugars, 0.2g salt

With its creamy sauce and generous helping of roast vegetables, this pasta dish will satisfy the heartiest of appetites.

INGREDIENTS

4 courgettes, roughly chopped

2½ tbsp olive oil

1 onion, finely chopped

1 garlic clove, crushed

800 g/1 lb 12 oz canned chopped tomatoes

6 sun-dried tomatoes, chopped

225 ml/8 fl oz vegetable stock

½ tsp dried oregano

280 g/10 oz dried rigatoni pasta

125 g/4½ oz vegetarian mascarpone cheese

salt and pepper

large handful of fresh basil leaves, torn into pieces

1. Preheat the oven to 200°C/400°F/Gas Mark 6. Place the courgettes and 1½ tablespoons of the oil in a large ovenproof dish. Toss together and spread out in a single layer. Roast in the preheated oven for 15–20 minutes until tender and lightly browned.

2. Meanwhile, heat the remaining oil in a saucepan. Add the onion and garlic and cook very gently for 5 minutes until soft. Add the canned tomatoes, sun-dried tomatoes, stock and oregano. Simmer for 10 minutes until the liquid has reduced slightly.

3. Bring a large saucepan of lightly salted water to the boil. Add the rigatoni, bring back to the boil and cook for 11–13 minutes, or until tender but still firm to the bite. Drain well, then return to the pan.

4. Add the mascarpone cheese to the hot sauce and stir until melted and smooth. Season well with salt and pepper. Add to the pasta with the roasted courgettes and the basil leaves. Toss together until the pasta is well coated in sauce. Serve immediately.

1

2

4

HEALTHY HINT
For a reduced-
fat version, roast
the courgettes on
a non-stick
baking tray
without oil and
replace the
cheese with
vegetarian low-fat
soft cheese.

Griddled Courgette & Feta Pizza

 MAKES: 2 pizzas

 PREP TIME: 20 minutes plus rising

 COOKING TIME: 15–20 minutes

nutritional information per pizza	996 kcals, 42g fat, 20g sat fat, 10g total sugars, 8.6g salt

However easy it is to send out for pizza, you can't beat the taste and texture of the dough when you make it yourself.

INGREDIENTS

basic pizza dough
300 g/10½ oz strong white flour, plus extra for dusting
1 tsp easy-blend dried yeast
1½ tsp salt
175 ml/6 fl oz hand-hot water
1 tbsp olive oil, plus extra for kneading

topping
1 tbsp olive oil
1 garlic clove, crushed
1 large courgette, sliced lengthways
200 g/7 oz ready-prepared tomato pizza sauce
250 g/9 oz vegetarian feta cheese, drained and crumbled
salt and pepper
fresh mint leaves, roughly torn, to garnish

1. Sift the flour into a mixing bowl and add the yeast and salt, making a small well in the top. Mix the water and oil together and pour into the bowl, using a round-bladed knife to gradually combine all the flour to make a sticky dough.

2. Lightly flour the work surface and your hands and knead the dough for about 10 minutes, until it is smooth and elastic.

3. Cover the dough with some lightly oiled clingfilm or a damp tea towel and leave to rise for about an hour, or until it has doubled in size.

4. Knock back the dough by gently kneading for about a minute, then divide into two balls. To roll out the dough, flatten each ball, then, using a rolling pin, roll out on a lightly floured work surface, giving a quarter turn between each roll.

5. Preheat the oven to 220°C/425°F/Gas Mark 7. Place the pizza bases on two baking trays, using a rolling pin to transfer them from the work surface.

6. Heat the oil in a griddle pan over a medium heat. Add the garlic and courgette and cook over a medium heat for 4–5 minutes, turning regularly, until softened and chargrilled. Remove with a slotted spoon and drain on kitchen paper.

7. Divide the pizza sauce between the two pizza bases, spreading almost to the edges. Place the courgette slices on the pizza bases, scatter with the cheese and season to taste with salt and pepper. Bake in the preheated oven for 10–12 minutes, or until the cheese is turning golden and the bases are crisp underneath. Garnish with the fresh mint and serve immediately.

New Potato, Feta & Herb Frittata

 SERVES 4   PREP TIME: 10 minutes   COOKING TIME: 30–35 minutes

nutritional information per serving	273 kcals, 19g fat, 8g sat fat, 1.5g total sugars, 1.5g salt

This chunky omelette is delicious cold as well as hot, so it's perfect for picnics and packed lunches.

INGREDIENTS

250 g/9 oz new potatoes, scrubbed

85 g/3 oz baby spinach leaves

5 eggs

1 tbsp chopped fresh dill, plus extra to garnish

1 tbsp snipped fresh chives, plus extra to garnish

115 g/4 oz vegetarian feta cheese, crumbled

10 g/¼ oz butter

1 tbsp olive oil

salt and pepper

1. Bring a saucepan of lightly salted water to the boil, add the potatoes, bring back to the boil and cook for 25 minutes until tender. Place the spinach in a colander and drain the potatoes over the top to wilt the spinach. Set aside until cool enough to handle.

2. Cut the potatoes lengthways into 5-mm/¼-in thick slices. Squeeze the excess water from the spinach leaves. Preheat the grill to high.

3. Lightly beat the eggs, dill and chives together. Season with pepper and add 85 g/3 oz of the cheese. Heat the butter and oil in a 20-cm/8-inch frying pan until melted and foaming. Add the potato slices and spinach and cook, stirring, for 1 minute. Pour the egg and cheese mixture over the top.

4. Cook, stirring, over a moderate heat for 1 minute until half set, then continue to cook for a further 2–3 minutes, without stirring, until set and golden brown underneath. Sprinkle the remaining cheese over the top, place under the preheated grill and cook for 2 minutes until golden brown on top. Serve hot or cold, sprinkled with chives and dill.

1

3

4

SOMETHING DIFFERENT

This frittata is a great way of using up leftover boiled, baked or roasted potatoes. Cut them into chunky pieces if they are too crumbly to slice.

Bean & Vegetable Chilli

 SERVES 4

 PREP TIME:
10 minutes

 COOKING TIME:
20 minutes

nutritional information
per serving

180 kcals, 1.5g fat, 0.2g sat fat, 14g total sugars, 1.4g salt

This must be one of the most popular dishes to serve a crowd. Take care not to go mad with the chilli – just have your favourite chilli sauce available so everyone can adjust the heat level to suit.

INGREDIENTS

4 tbsp vegetable stock
1 onion, roughly chopped
1 green pepper, deseeded and finely chopped
1 red pepper, deseeded and finely chopped
1 tsp finely chopped garlic
1 tsp finely chopped fresh ginger
2 tsp ground cumin
½ tsp chilli powder
2 tbsp tomato purée
400 g/14 oz canned chopped tomatoes
400 g/14 oz canned kidney beans, drained and rinsed
400 g/14 oz canned black-eyed beans, drained and rinsed
salt and pepper
tortilla chips, to serve

1. Heat the stock in a large saucepan, add the onion and peppers and simmer for 5 minutes, or until softened.

2. Stir in the garlic, ginger, cumin, chilli powder, tomato purée and tomatoes. Season to taste with salt and pepper and simmer for 10 minutes.

3. Stir in all the beans and simmer for a further 5 minutes, or until heated through. Serve immediately with tortilla chips.

Quinoa with Roasted Vegetables

 SERVES 2  PREP TIME: 10 minutes COOKING TIME: 40–45 minutes

nutritional information per serving	418 kcals, 23g fat, 2g sat fat, 14g total sugars, 0.1g salt

Quinoa (pronounced keen-wah) is an ancient grain originating from South America.

INGREDIENTS

2 peppers (any colour), deseeded and cut into chunky pieces

1 large courgette, cut into chunks

1 small fennel bulb, cut into slim wedges

1 tbsp olive oil

2 tsp very finely chopped fresh rosemary

1 tsp chopped fresh thyme

100 g/3½ oz quinoa

350 ml/12 fl oz vegetable stock

2 garlic cloves, crushed

3 tbsp chopped fresh flat leaf parsley

40 g/1½ oz pine nuts, toasted

salt and pepper

1. Preheat the oven to 200°C/400°F/Gas Mark 6. Place the peppers, courgette and fennel in a roasting tin large enough to hold the vegetables in a single layer.

2. Drizzle the olive oil over the vegetables and scatter with the rosemary and thyme. Season well with salt and pepper and mix well with clean hands. Roast for 25–30 minutes until tender and lightly charred.

3. Meanwhile, place the quinoa, stock and garlic in a saucepan. Bring to the boil, cover and simmer for 12–15 minutes until tender and most of the stock has been absorbed.

4. Remove the vegetables from the oven. Tip the quinoa into the roasting tin. Add the parsley and pine nuts and toss together. Serve warm or cold.

1

2

3

SOMETHING
DIFFERENT

If you're unable
to buy highly
nutritious quinoa
(although it's
a very popular
grain these days)
use brown
basmati rice
instead.

Lattice Flan

 SERVES 8   PREP TIME: 30 minutes plus chilling   COOKING TIME: 60 minutes

nutritional information per serving	483 kcals, 32g fat, 17g sat fat, 3g total sugars, 1.1g salt

The perfect combination of spinach and ricotta encased in crispy shortcrust pastry.

INGREDIENTS

rich shortcrust pastry
350 g/12 oz plain flour, plus extra for dusting
pinch of salt
175 g/6 oz butter, diced, plus extra for greasing
2 egg yolks
6 tbsp ice-cold water

filling
450 g/1 lb frozen spinach, thawed
2 tbsp olive oil
1 large onion, chopped
2 garlic cloves, finely chopped
2 eggs, lightly beaten
225 g/8 oz vegetarian ricotta cheese
55 g/2 oz freshly grated vegetarian Parmesan-style cheese
pinch of freshly grated nutmeg
salt and pepper

1. To make the pastry, sift the flour with the salt into a bowl. Add the butter and rub into the flour with your fingertips until the mixture resembles fine breadcrumbs. Beat the egg yolks with the water in a small bowl. Sprinkle the liquid over the flour mixture and combine with a round-bladed knife to form a dough. Shape into a ball, wrap in foil and chill in the refrigerator for 30 minutes.

2. To make the filling, drain the spinach and squeeze out as much moisture as possible. Heat the oil in a large, heavy-based frying pan over a medium heat. Add the onion and cook, stirring frequently, for 5 minutes, or until softened. Add the garlic and spinach and cook, stirring occasionally, for 10 minutes. Remove from the heat and leave to cool slightly, then beat in the eggs (reserving a little for glazing), the ricotta and the grated cheese. Season to taste with salt and pepper and nutmeg.

3. Preheat the oven to 200°C/400°F/Gas Mark 6. Lightly grease a 23-cm/9-inch loose-based flan tin. Roll out two-thirds of the dough on a lightly floured work surface and use to line the tin. Spoon in the spinach mixture, spreading it evenly over the base.

4. Roll out the remaining dough on a lightly floured work surface and cut into 5-mm/¼-inch strips. Arrange the strips in a lattice pattern on top of the flan, pressing the ends securely to seal. Trim any excess pastry. Brush with the egg to glaze and bake in the preheated oven for 45 minutes, or until golden brown. Transfer to a wire rack to cool slightly before removing from the tin.

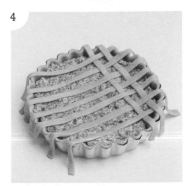

Mixed Nut Roast with Cranberry & Red Wine Sauce

 MAKES
1 loaf

 PREP TIME:
15 minutes

 COOKING TIME:
30 minutes

nutritional information per loaf	711 kcals, 45g fat, 8.5g sat fat, 31g total sugars, 0.7g salt

Serve with roast carrots, parsnips and potatoes for an alternative Christmas feast.

INGREDIENTS

2 tbsp butter, plus extra for greasing
2 garlic cloves, chopped
1 large onion, chopped
50 g/1¾ oz pine nuts, toasted
75 g/2¾ oz hazelnuts, toasted
50 g/1¾ oz walnuts, ground
50 g/1¾ oz cashew nuts, ground
100 g/3½ oz fresh wholemeal breadcrumbs
1 egg, lightly beaten
2 tbsp chopped fresh thyme, plus extra sprigs to garnish
250 ml/9 fl oz vegetable stock
salt and pepper

cranberry & red wine sauce
175 g/6 oz fresh cranberries
100 g/3½ oz caster sugar
300 ml/10 fl oz red wine
1 cinnamon stick

1. Preheat the oven to 180°C/350°F/Gas Mark 4. Grease a loaf tin and line it with greaseproof paper. Melt the butter in a saucepan over a medium heat. Add the garlic and onion and cook, stirring, for about 3 minutes. Remove the pan from the heat. Grind the pine nuts and hazelnuts. Stir all the nuts into the pan and add the breadcrumbs, egg, thyme, stock and salt and pepper to taste.

2. Spoon the mixture into the loaf tin and level the surface. Cook in the centre of the preheated oven for 30 minutes or until cooked through and golden. The loaf is cooked when a skewer inserted into the centre comes out clean.

3. Halfway through the cooking time, make the cranberry and red wine sauce. Put all the ingredients in a saucepan and bring to the boil. Reduce the heat and simmer, stirring occasionally, for 15 minutes.

4. Remove the nut roast from the oven and turn out. Garnish with sprigs of thyme and serve with the cranberry and red wine sauce.

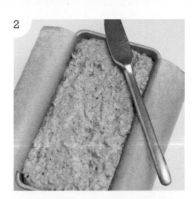

Mushrooms with Garlic & Spring Onions 98

Hot & Sour Courgettes 100

Braised Peas with Lettuce & Tarragon 102

Roast Fennel with Cherry Tomatoes & Rosemary 104

Spicy Chickpeas 106

Stir-fried Broccoli 108

Spicy Pak Choi with Sesame Sauce 110

Mexican Rice 112

Plaited Poppy Seed Bread 114

Cherry Tomato, Rosemary & Sea Salt Focaccia 116

Pesto & Olive Soda Bread 118

Green Leaf & Herb Chutney with Olives 120

Apricot Buzz 122

Celery & Apple Revitalizer 124

Accompaniments

Mushrooms with Garlic & Spring Onions

 SERVES 4

 PREP TIME:
10 minutes
plus cooling

 COOKING TIME:
1½ hours

nutritional information per serving	80 kcals, 6g fat, 1g sat fat, 2g total sugars, trace salt

There may seem to be a huge amount of garlic in this recipe but don't worry, when you roast whole bulbs in the oven in this way they become milder, sweeter and deliciously caramelized.

INGREDIENTS

2 garlic bulbs

2 tbsp olive oil

350 g/12 oz assorted mushrooms, such as chestnut, open-cap and chanterelles, halved if large

1 tbsp chopped fresh parsley

8 spring onions, cut into 2.5-cm/1-inch lengths

salt and pepper

1. Preheat the oven to 180°C/350°F/Gas Mark 4. Slice off the tops of the garlic bulbs and press down to loosen the cloves. Place them in an ovenproof dish and season with salt and pepper to taste. Drizzle 2 teaspoons of the oil over the bulbs and roast for 30 minutes. Remove from the oven and drizzle with 1 teaspoon of the remaining oil. Return to the oven and roast for an additional 45 minutes. Remove the garlic from the oven and, when cool enough to handle, peel the cloves.

2. Tip the oil from the dish into a heavy-based frying pan. Add the remaining oil and heat. Add the mushrooms and cook over a medium heat, stirring frequently, for 4 minutes.

3. Add the garlic cloves, parsley and spring onions and cook, stirring frequently, for 5 minutes. Season with salt and pepper to taste and serve immediately.

GOES WELL WITH
Serve on toasted
ciabatta bread or
with scrambled
eggs.

Hot & Sour Courgettes

 SERVES 4

 PREP TIME:
30 minutes

 COOKING TIME:
5 minutes

nutritional information per serving	86 kcals, 7g fat, 1.5g sat fat, 4g total sugars, 1.9g salt

In a traditional Sichuan style, this is just one more way to serve the humble courgette.

INGREDIENTS

2 large courgettes, thinly sliced

1 tsp salt

2 tbsp groundnut oil

1 tsp Sichuan peppercorns, crushed

½–1 red chilli, deseeded and sliced into thin strips

1 large garlic clove, thinly sliced

½ tsp finely chopped fresh ginger

1 tbsp rice vinegar

1 tbsp light soy sauce

2 tsp sugar

1 spring onion, green part included, thinly sliced

a few drops of sesame oil and 1 tsp sesame seeds, to garnish

1. Put the courgette slices in a large colander and toss with the salt. Cover with a plate and put a weight on top. Leave to drain for 20 minutes. Rinse off the salt and spread out the slices on kitchen paper to dry.

2. Preheat a wok over a high heat and add the groundnut oil. Add the Sichuan peppercorns, chilli, garlic and ginger. Fry for about 20 seconds until the garlic is just beginning to colour.

3. Add the courgette slices and toss in the oil. Add the rice vinegar, soy sauce and sugar, and stir-fry for 2 minutes. Add the spring onion and fry for 30 seconds. Garnish with the sesame oil and seeds, and serve immediately.

1

2

3

COOK'S NOTE
Don't miss out on salting the courgettes as this helps to draw out the excess water that can make the dish soggy.

Braised Peas with Lettuce & Tarragon

 SERVES 4

 PREP TIME: 5 minutes

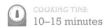 COOKING TIME: 10–15 minutes

nutritional information per serving	162 kcals, 8g fat, 3g sat fat, 3g total sugars, trace salt

Transform humble peas into a side dish fit for a dinner party with this quick recipe.

INGREDIENTS

15 g/½ oz butter
1 tbsp olive oil
1 leek, thinly sliced
2 tsp plain flour
250 ml/9 fl oz vegetable stock
375 g/13 oz fresh or frozen peas
2 large Little Gem lettuces, sliced
3 tbsp chopped fresh tarragon
1 tbsp lemon juice
salt and pepper

1. Heat the butter and oil in a large saucepan. Add the leek, cover and cook over a low heat for 5 minutes until soft. Stir in the flour, then gradually stir in the stock.

2. Add the peas, increase the heat, cover and simmer for 4 minutes. Add the lettuce without stirring it in, cover and simmer for a further 2 minutes until the vegetables are tender.

3. Stir the lettuce, tarragon and lemon juice into the peas. Season with salt and pepper and serve immediately.

1

2

3

SOMETHING
DIFFERENT
To vary the
flavour, replace
the tarragon
with mint or the
Gem lettuce with
chicory.

Roast Fennel with Cherry Tomatoes & Rosemary

 SERVES 4 PREP TIME: 5 minutes 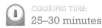 COOKING TIME: 25–30 minutes

nutritional information per serving	100 kcals, 7.5g fat, 1g sat fat, 3g total sugars, 0.2g salt

A lovely side dish for the summer months when these vegetables are at their cheapest and best.

INGREDIENTS

4 fennel bulbs, cut into slim wedges
2 tbsp olive oil
6 tbsp dry white wine
2 garlic cloves, crushed
2 tsp chopped fresh rosemary
200 g/7 oz cherry tomatoes
16 stoned black olives
2 tbsp chopped fresh parsley
salt and pepper

1. Preheat the oven to 200°C/400°F/Gas Mark 6. Place the fennel in a roasting tin large enough to hold it in a single layer. Mix the oil, 2 tablespoons of the wine, the garlic and rosemary together. Pour the mixture over the fennel, season with salt and pepper and toss together.

2. Roast in the preheated oven for 15–20 minutes until almost tender and lightly browned. Scatter the tomatoes and olives over the fennel. Pour over the remaining wine, then return to the oven for 8–10 minutes until the tomatoes are soft and the skins have burst. Toss with the parsley and serve warm or cold.

GOES WELL WITH
To turn this side
dish into a light
meal, toss with
couscous and
toasted pine nuts
or with pasta
and grated
vegetarian
Parmesan-style
cheese.

Spicy Chickpeas

 SERVES 4   PREP TIME: 10 minutes  COOKING TIME: 10–12 minutes

nutritional information per serving	190 kcals, 2.2g fat, 0.2g sat fat, 10g total sugars, 0.4g salt

This traditional Indian dish goes really well with plain boiled rice and a cucumber raita.

INGREDIENTS

400 g/14 oz canned chickpeas, drained
2 potatoes, diced
2 tbsp tamarind paste
6 tbsp water
1 tsp chilli powder
2 tsp sugar
1 onion, chopped
salt

to garnish
1 tomato, sliced
2 fresh green chillies, chopped
2–3 tbsp chopped fresh coriander

1. Place the drained chickpeas in a large bowl.

2. Place the potatoes in a saucepan of water and boil for 10-12 minutes or until cooked through. Drain and set aside.

3. Mix the tamarind paste and water together in a small bowl.

4. Add the chilli powder, sugar and 1 teaspoon of salt to the tamarind paste mixture and mix together. Pour the mixture over the chickpeas.

5. Add the onion and the diced potatoes, and stir to mix.

6. Transfer to a serving bowl and garnish with tomato, chillies and chopped coriander. Serve immediately.

COOK'S NOTE
Tamarind paste
is sold in slabs
and may be
available in your
supermarket,
otherwise check
out Asian stores.
It has a unique
sour flavour
which cannot be
substituted.

Stir-fried Broccoli

 SERVES 4

 PREP TIME:
5 minutes

 COOKING TIME:
8–10 minutes

nutritional information per serving	121 kcals, 7.5g fat, 1g sat fat, 6g total sugars, 1.3g salt

Broccoli served this way will tempt everyone to try this great dish, which is equally delicious made with cauliflower or a combination of the two.

INGREDIENTS

2 tbsp vegetable oil
2 broccoli heads, cut into florets
2 tbsp soy sauce
1 tsp cornflour
1 tbsp caster sugar
1 tsp grated fresh ginger
1 garlic clove, crushed
pinch of dried red pepper flakes
1 tsp toasted sesame seeds, to garnish

1. Heat the oil in a large preheated wok or frying pan over high heat until almost smoking. Add the broccoli and stir-fry for 4–5 minutes. Reduce the heat to medium.

2. Combine the soy sauce, cornflour, sugar, ginger, garlic and red pepper flakes in a small bowl. Add the mixture to the broccoli and cook, stirring constantly, for 2–3 minutes until the sauce thickens slightly.

3. Transfer to a warmed serving dish, garnish with the sesame seeds and serve immediately.

1

2

2

HEALTHY HINT
If you prefer, you could steam the broccoli for 3-4 minutes until tender.

Spicy Pak Choi with Sesame Sauce

 SERVES 4   PREP TIME: 10 minutes   COOKING TIME: 8–10 minutes

nutritional information per serving	163 kcals, 14g fat, 2g sat fat, 4.5g total sugars, 1.7g salt

Pak Choi is also known as Bok Choi and is a member of the cabbage family. Choose the smaller more tender ones with perky leaves and unblemished stalks.

INGREDIENTS

2 tsp groundnut or vegetable oil
1 red chilli, deseeded and thinly sliced
1 garlic clove, thinly sliced
5 small pak choi, quartered
100 ml/3½ fl oz vegetable stock

sauce
25 g/1 oz sesame seeds
2 tbsp dark soy sauce
2 tsp soft light brown sugar
1 garlic clove, crushed
3 tbsp sesame oil

1. For the sesame sauce, toast the sesame seeds in a dry frying pan set over a medium heat, stirring until lightly browned. Remove from the heat and cool slightly. Transfer to a pestle and mortar. Add the soy sauce, sugar and crushed garlic and pound to a coarse paste. Stir in the sesame oil.

2. Heat the groundnut oil in a wok or large frying pan. Add the chilli and sliced garlic and stir-fry for 20–30 seconds. Add the pak choi and stir-fry for 5 minutes, adding the stock a little at a time to prevent sticking.

3. Transfer the pak choi to a warmed dish, drizzle the sesame sauce over the top and serve immediately.

1

2

2

COOK'S NOTE
This sesame sauce
recipe is a great
standby to keep
in the fridge
as it's excellent
poured over most
steamed vegetables.

Mexican Rice

nutritional information per serving	210 kcals, 1g fat, 0.1g sat fat, 4g total sugars, trace salt

Colourful tomato-flavoured rice is great for serving to the family with a wide selection of main dishes.

INGREDIENTS

1 onion, chopped

400 g/14 oz plum tomatoes, peeled, deseeded and chopped

250 ml/9 fl oz vegetable stock

200 g/7 oz long-grain rice

salt and pepper

1. Put the onion and tomatoes in a food processor and process to a smooth purée. Scrape the purée into a saucepan, pour in the stock and bring to the boil over a medium heat, stirring occasionally.

2. Add the rice and stir once, then reduce the heat, cover and simmer for 20–25 minutes until all the liquid has been absorbed and the rice is tender. Season to taste with salt and pepper and serve immediately.

1

1

2

SOMETHING
DIFFERENT
Serve with your
favourite chilli
sauce if you like
some heat.

Plaited Poppy Seed Bread

 MAKES
1 loaf

 PREP TIME:
20 minutes
plus rising

 COOKING TIME:
30–35 minutes

nutritional information per loaf	1342 kcals, 85g fat, 14g sat fat, 56g total sugars, 4.6g salt

Ring the changes with this recipe and use other seeds such as sesame, onion or pumpkin instead of poppy.

INGREDIENTS

225 g/8 oz strong white flour, plus extra for dusting
1 tsp salt
2 tbsp skimmed milk powder
1½ tbsp caster sugar
1 tsp easy-blend dried yeast
175 ml/6 fl oz lukewarm water
2 tbsp vegetable oil, plus extra for greasing
5 tbsp poppy seeds

topping
1 egg yolk
1 tbsp milk
1 tbsp caster sugar
2 tbsp poppy seeds

1. Sift the flour and salt together into a bowl and stir in the milk powder, sugar and yeast. Make a well in the centre, pour in the water and oil and stir until the dough begins to come together. Add the poppy seeds and knead until fully combined and the dough leaves the side of the bowl. Turn out onto a lightly floured surface and knead well for about 10 minutes, until smooth and elastic.

2. Brush a bowl with oil. Shape the dough into a ball, put it in the bowl, and place the bowl in a plastic bag or cover with a damp tea towel and leave to rise in a warm place for 1 hour, or until doubled in volume.

3. Oil a baking sheet. Turn out the dough onto a lightly floured surface, and knead for 1–2 minutes. Divide into three equal pieces and shape each into a rope 25–30 cm/10–12 inches long. Place the ropes side by side and press together at one end. Plait the dough, pinch the other end together and tuck underneath.

4. Put the loaf on the prepared baking sheet, cover and leave to rise in a warm place for 30 minutes. Meanwhile, preheat the oven to 200°C/400°F/Gas Mark 6.

5. For the topping, beat the egg yolk with the milk and sugar. Brush the egg glaze over the top of the loaf and sprinkle with the poppy seeds. Bake in the preheated oven for 30–35 minutes, until golden brown. Transfer to a wire rack and leave to cool.

Cherry Tomato, Rosemary & Sea Salt Focaccia

 MAKES
1 loaf

 PREP TIME:
20 minutes
plus rising

 COOKING TIME:
25–30 minutes

nutritional information per loaf	1742 kcals, 60g fat, 9g sat fat, 16g total sugars, 11g salt

A simplified version of the classic loaf studded with roasted cherry tomatoes and aromatic rosemary.

INGREDIENTS

5 tbsp olive oil, plus extra for greasing

2 garlic cloves, crushed

350 g/12 oz strong white flour, plus extra for kneading

1 sachet easy-blend dried yeast

2 tsp table salt

1 tsp caster sugar

225 ml/8 fl oz lukewarm water

2 tsp finely chopped fresh rosemary

200–225g/7–8 oz ripe red cherry tomatoes

¼ tsp flaky sea salt

1. Mix 2 tablespoons of the oil and all of the garlic. Set aside. Mix the flour, yeast, table salt and sugar together in a large bowl. Add the remaining oil and water. Mix to a dough. Turn out onto a lightly floured surface and knead for 10 minutes until smooth and elastic, then knead in 1 tablespoon of the garlic-flavoured oil.

2. Oil a rectangular baking tin measuring approximately 17 x 25 cm/ 6½ x10 inches and at least 4 cm/1½ inches deep. Press the dough over the base of the tin with your hands. Brush with the remaining garlic oil, then scatter over the rosemary. Cover loosely with clingfilm and set aside in a warm place for about 1 hour until puffed up and doubled in size.

3. Preheat the oven to 230°C/450°F/Gas Mark 8. Scatter the tomatoes over the focaccia (squeeze in as many as you can) and press them into the base of the dough. Sprinkle with the sea salt. Place in the preheated oven and immediately reduce the temperature to 200°C/400°F/Gas Mark 6. Bake for 25–30 minutes until golden brown and the centre sounds hollow when tapped. Turn out onto a wire rack to cool. Serve warm or cold.

1

2

3

COOK'S NOTE
If you don't have a deep baking tin, press out the dough to roughly the same size on an oiled baking tray.

Pesto & Olive Soda Bread

 MAKES
1 loaf

 PREP TIME:
15 minutes

 COOKING TIME:
30–35 minutes

nutritional information per loaf	2156 kcals, 43g fat, 4g sat fat, 21g total sugars, 6.7g salt

If you're not confident about baking with yeast try this recipe. You'll be delighted with the result. Use one of the many ready-made pestos available in shops or make your own. Either way you will have a loaf to be proud of.

INGREDIENTS

olive oil, for greasing
250 g/9 oz plain flour
250 g/9 oz wholemeal flour
1 tsp bicarbonate of soda
½ tsp salt
3 tbsp pesto
300 ml/10 fl oz buttermilk, (approx)
55 g/2 oz pitted green olives, roughly chopped
milk, for glazing

1. Preheat the oven to 200°C/400°F/Gas Mark 6 and line and grease a baking tray. Sift the flours, bicarbonate of soda and salt into a bowl, adding back any bran from the sieve.

2. Mix the pesto and buttermilk. Stir into the flour with the olives, mixing to a soft dough. Add more liquid if needed.

3. Shape the dough into a 20-cm/8-inch round and place on the baking tray. Flatten slightly and cut a deep cross with a sharp knife.

4. Brush with milk and bake in the preheated oven for 30–35 minutes, until golden brown. The loaf should sound hollow when tapped underneath. Transfer to a wire rack to cool.

COOK'S NOTE
Soda bread
doesn't keep
like yeast-risen
recipes so bake
fresh on the day
you want it.

Green Leaf & Herb Chutney with Olives

 SERVES 4

 PREP TIME:
10 minutes
plus cooling

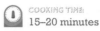 COOKING TIME:
15–20 minutes

nutritional information per serving	95 kcals, 9.5g fat, 1.5g sat fat, 1g total sugars, 0.3g salt

With a vibrant green colour and zingy combination of herbs and spices, this is perfect spread on bread but equally good as a dip or accompaniment to main course dishes.

INGREDIENTS

225 g/8 oz fresh baby spinach leaves

handful of celery leaves

3 tbsp olive oil

2–3 garlic cloves, crushed

1 tsp cumin seeds

6–8 black olives, stoned and finely chopped

1 large bunch of fresh flat-leaf parsley leaves, finely chopped

1 large bunch of fresh coriander leaves, finely chopped

1 tsp Spanish smoked paprika

juice of ½ lemon

salt and pepper

toasted flat bread or crusty bread and black olives, to serve

1. Place the spinach and celery leaves in a steamer and steam until tender. Refresh the leaves under cold running water, drain well and squeeze out the excess water. Place the steamed leaves on a wooden chopping board and chop to a pulp.

2. Heat 2 tablespoons of the oil in a heavy-based casserole. Add the garlic and cumin seeds, then cook over a medium heat for 1–2 minutes, stirring, until they emit a nutty aroma. Stir in the olives with the parsley and coriander and add the paprika.

3. Toss in the pulped spinach and celery and cook over a low heat, stirring occasionally, for 10 minutes until the mixture is smooth and compact. Season with salt and pepper to taste and leave to cool.

4. Tip the mixture into a bowl and bind with the remaining oil and the lemon juice. Serve with toasted flat bread or crusty bread and olives.

Apricot Buzz

 SERVES 2   PREP TIME: 5 minutes   COOKING TIME: No cooking

nutritional information per serving	52 kcals, 0.2g fat, 0g sat fat, 11g total sugars, trace salt

When apricots are ripe and bursting with flavour, this Asian inspired "mocktail" will really go down well. Serve with ice on a warm summer morning.

INGREDIENTS

6 apricots
1 orange
1 fresh lemon grass stalk
2-cm/¾-inch piece fresh ginger, peeled
ice cubes, to serve

1. Halve and stone the apricots. Peel the orange, leaving some of the white pith. Cut the lemon grass into chunks.

2. Place the apricots, orange, lemon grass and ginger in a food processor or juicer and blend all the ingredients together. Pour the mixture into glasses, add ice and serve.

1

2

2

COOK'S NOTE
Using a teaspoon to scrape the skin from fresh ginger makes the job easier.

Celery & Apple Revitalizer

 SERVES 2   PREP TIME: 5 minutes   COOKING TIME: No cooking

nutritional information per serving	225 kcals, 12g fat, 7g sat fat, 20g total sugars, 0.5g salt

A milkshake that does you good! Celery and apple are the perfect combination in this drink that is great on hot summer days. Serve in tall glasses with strips of celery to decorate.

INGREDIENTS

115 g/4 oz celery, chopped

1 eating apple, peeled, cored and diced

600 ml/1 pint milk

pinch of sugar (optional)

salt (optional)

strips of celery, for decorating

1. Place the celery, apple and milk in a blender and process until thoroughly combined.

2. Stir in the sugar and some salt, if using. Pour into chilled glasses, decorate with strips of celery and serve.

1

2

2

HEALTHY HINT
For a thicker
drink use half
milk and half
liquid yogurt.

Index

apples
  Caramelized Apple & Blue
    Cheese Salad 48
  Celery & Apple Revitalizer 124
Apricot Buzz 122
asparagus
  Stir-fried Rice with Green
    Vegetables 74
aubergines
  Aubergine Pâté 10
  Aubergine, Pepper & Basil
    Crêpe Rolls 52
  Mediterranean Vegetables with
    Feta & Olives 78
  Melting Mozzarella Bagels 50
  Mini Roast Vegetable
    Skewers 22
avocados
  Avocado Salad with Lime
    Dressing 38
  Spicy Avocado Dip 18

basil
  Aubergine, Pepper & Basil
    Crêpe Rolls 52
  Pea & Herb Soup with Basil Oil 8
  Stir-fried Rice with Green
    Vegetables 74
beans
  Bean & Vegetable Chilli 88
  Grilled Halloumi Kebabs on
    Fennel & White Bean Salad 34
  Smoky Mushroom & Coriander
    Burgers 70
  White Bean Soup 28
beansprouts
  Crunchy Thai-style Salad 42
beetroot
  Glazed Beetroot & Egg
    Sourdough Toasties 54
Blue Cheese & Herb Pâté 26
Braised Peas with Lettuce &
    Tarragon 102
bread
  Aubergine Pâté 10
  Cherry Tomato, Rosemary &
    Sea Salt Focaccia 116
  Glazed Beetroot & Egg
    Sourdough Toasties 54

Greek Salad Crostini 60
Melting Mozzarella Bagels 50
Pesto & Olive Soda Bread 118
Plaited Poppy Seed Bread 114
Roast Squash Soup with Cheese
    Toasties 24
broccoli
  Stir-fried Broccoli 108
  Vegetable & Corn Chowder 16

Caramelized Apple & Blue
    Cheese Salad 48
cauliflower
  Vegetable Pakoras 30
Celery & Apple Revitalizer 124
cheese
  Aubergine, Pepper & Basil
    Crêpe Rolls 52
  Blue Cheese & Herb Pâté 26
  Caramelized Apple & Blue
    Cheese Salad 48
  Eggs Florentine 40
  Feta, Lemon & Herb Dip 14
  Greek Salad Crostini 60
  Griddled Courgette &
    Feta Pizza 84
  Grilled Halloumi Kebabs on
    Fennel & White Bean Salad 34
  Lattice Flan 92
  Mediterranean Vegetables with
    Feta & Olives 78
  Melting Mozzarella Bagels 50
  New Potato, Feta & Herb
    Frittata 86
  Pasta with Two Cheeses &
    Walnuts 76
  Rigatoni with Roast Courgette,
    Tomato & Mascarpone
    Sauce 82
  Roast Squash Soup with Cheese
    Toasties 24
  Vegetable & Corn Chowder 16
Cherry Tomato, Rosemary & Sea
    Salt Focaccia 116
chickpeas
  Spicy Chickpeas 106
chillies
  Bean & Vegetable Chilli 88

Hot & Sour Courgettes 100
Spicy Chickpeas 106
Spicy Lentil Soup 20
Spicy Pak Choi with Sesame
    Sauce 110
Spicy Polenta with Poached
    Eggs 62
Thai Tofu Cakes with
    Chilli Dip 58
coriander
  Green Leaf & Herb Chutney
    with Olives 120
  Smoky Mushroom & Coriander
    Burgers 70
  Vegetable Pakoras 30
corn
  Teriyaki Tofu Stir-fry 80
  Thai Vermicelli Soup 32
  Vegetable & Corn Chowder 16
courgettes
  Courgette Fritters with Eggs &
    Caramelized Onions 46
  Griddled Courgette &
    Feta Pizza 84
  Hot & Sour Courgettes 100
  Mini Roast Vegetable
    Skewers 22
  Rigatoni with Roast Courgette,
    Tomato & Mascarpone
    Sauce 82
  Spicy Courgette Soup with
    Rice & Lime 12
  Stir-fried Rice with Green
    Vegetables 74
Couscous Salad with Roasted
    Butternut Squash 64
Couscous with Roast Cherry
    Tomatoes & Pine Nuts 44
cranberries
  Blue Cheese & Herb Pâté 26
  Mixed Nut Roast with
    Cranberry & Red Wine
    Sauce 94
Creamy Mushroom Pancakes 56
crème fraîche
  Pea & Herb Soup with Basil Oil 8
  Roast Squash Soup with Cheese
    Toasties 24

Crunchy Thai-style Salad 42
cucumber
  Couscous Salad with Roasted
    Butternut Squash 64
  Greek Salad Crostini 60

eggs
  Courgette Fritters with Eggs &
    Caramelized Onions 46
  Eggs Florentine 40
  Glazed Beetroot & Egg
    Sourdough Toasties 54
  Lattice Flan 92
  New Potato, Feta & Herb
    Frittata 86
  Spicy Polenta with Poached
    Eggs 62
environmental concerns 5

fennel
  Grilled Halloumi Kebabs on
    Fennel & White Bean Salad 34
  Quinoa with Roasted
    Vegetables 90
  Roast Fennel with Cherry
    Tomatoes & Rosemary 104
Feta, Lemon & Herb Dip 14

garlic
  Lentil Bolognese 68
  Mushrooms with Garlic &
    Spring Onions 98
  Spicy Courgette Soup with
    Rice & Lime 12
ginger
  Apricot Buzz 122
  Hot & Sour Courgettes 100
  Stir-fried Broccoli 108
Glazed Beetroot & Egg
  Sourdough Toasties 54
Greek Salad Crostini 60
Green Leaf & Herb Chutney
  with Olives 120
Griddled Courgette &
  Feta Pizza 84
Grilled Halloumi Kebabs on
  Fennel & White Bean Salad 34

herbs
  Blue Cheese & Herb Pâté 26
  Feta, Lemon & Herb Dip 14
  Green Leaf & Herb Chutney
    with Olives 120
  Leek, Herb & Mushroom
    Risotto 72
  New Potato, Feta & Herb
    Frittata 86
  Pea & Herb Soup with Basil Oil 8
Hot & Sour Courgettes 100

Lattice Flan 92
Leek, Herb & Mushroom
  Risotto 72
lemons
  Feta, Lemon & Herb Dip 14
lentils
  Lentil Bolognese 68
  Spicy Lentil Soup 20
lettuce
  Braised Peas with Lettuce &
    Tarragon 102
  Crunchy Thai-style Salad 42
  Greek Salad Crostini 60
limes
  Avocado Salad with Lime
    Dressing 38
  Spicy Avocado Dip 18
  Spicy Courgette Soup with
    Rice & Lime 12

mangoes
  Crunchy Thai-style Salad 42
Mediterranean Vegetables with
  Feta & Olives 78
Melting Mozzarella Bagels 50
Mexican Rice 112
Mini Roast Vegetable Skewers 22
mint
  Couscous with Roast Cherry
    Tomatoes & Pine Nuts 44
  Feta, Lemon & Herb Dip 14
Mixed Nut Roast with Cranberry
  & Red Wine Sauce 94
mushrooms
  Creamy Mushroom Pancakes 56
  Eggs Florentine 40
  Leek, Herb & Mushroom
    Risotto 72

Mushrooms with Garlic &
  Spring Onions 98
Smoky Mushroom & Coriander
  Burgers 70
Thai Vermicelli Soup 32

New Potato, Feta & Herb
  Frittata 86
noodles
  Teriyaki Tofu Stir-fry 80
  Thai Vermicelli Soup 32
nuts
  Mixed Nut Roast with
    Cranberry & Red Wine
    Sauce 94

olives
  Green Leaf & Herb Chutney
    with Olives 120
  Mediterranean Vegetables with
    Feta & Olives 78
  Pesto & Olive Soda Bread 118
  Roast Fennel with Cherry
    Tomatoes & Rosemary 104
onions
  Courgette Fritters with Eggs &
    Caramelized Onions 46
  Mexican Rice 112
  Mushrooms with Garlic &
    Spring Onions 98
oranges
  Apricot Buzz 122

pak choi
  Spicy Pak Choi with Sesame
    Sauce 110
pancakes
  Aubergine, Pepper & Basil
    Crêpe Rolls 52
  Creamy Mushroom Pancakes 56
parsley
  Creamy Mushroom Pancakes 56
  Green Leaf & Herb Chutney
    with Olives 120
  White Bean Soup 28
pasta
  Lentil Bolognese 68
  Pasta with Two Cheeses &
    Walnuts 76

Rigatoni with Roast Courgette, Tomato & Mascarpone Sauce 82
White Bean Soup 28
peas
Braised Peas with Lettuce & Tarragon 102
Pea & Herb Soup with Basil Oil 8
peppers
Aubergine, Pepper & Basil Crêpe Rolls 52
Bean & Vegetable Chilli 88
Mediterranean Vegetables with Feta & Olives 78
Mini Roast Vegetable Skewers 22
Quinoa with Roasted Vegetables 90
Teriyaki Tofu Stir-fry 80
Pesto & Olive Soda Bread 118
pine nuts
Couscous with Roast Cherry Tomatoes & Pine Nuts 44
pizza
Griddled Courgette & Feta Pizza 84
Plaited Poppy Seed Bread 114
polenta
Spicy Polenta with Poached Eggs 62
potatoes
New Potato, Feta & Herb Frittata 86
Spicy Chickpeas 106
Vegetable & Corn Chowder 16

Quinoa with Roasted Vegetables 90

rice
Leek, Herb & Mushroom Risotto 72
Mexican Rice 112
Spicy Courgette Soup with Rice & Lime 12
Stir-fried Rice with Green Vegetables 74

Rigatoni with Roast Courgette, Tomato & Mascarpone Sauce 82
Roast Fennel with Cherry Tomatoes & Rosemary 104
Roast Squash Soup with Cheese Toasties 24
rosemary
Cherry Tomato, Rosemary & Sea Salt Focaccia 116
Roast Fennel with Cherry Tomatoes & Rosemary 104

salt
Cherry Tomato, Rosemary & Sea Salt Focaccia 116
seeds
Plaited Poppy Seed Bread 114
sesame
Hot & Sour Courgettes 100
Spicy Pak Choi with Sesame Sauce 110
Stir-fried Broccoli 108
Smoky Mushroom & Coriander Burgers 70
Spicy Avocado Dip 18
Spicy Chickpeas 106
Spicy Courgette Soup with Rice & Lime 12
Spicy Lentil Soup 20
Spicy Pak Choi with Sesame Sauce 110
Spicy Polenta with Poached Eggs 62
spinach
Eggs Florentine 40
Green Leaf & Herb Chutney with Olives 120
Lattice Flan 92
squash
Couscous Salad with Roasted Butternut Squash 64
Roast Squash Soup with Cheese Toasties 24
Stir-fried Broccoli 108
Stir-fried Rice with Green Vegetables 74
sweetcorn see corn

tamarind
Spicy Chickpeas 106
tarragon
Braised Peas with Lettuce & Tarragon 102
Teriyaki Tofu Stir-fry 80
Thai Tofu Cakes with Chilli Dip 58
Thai Vermicelli Soup 32
tofu
Teriyaki Tofu Stir-fry 80
Thai Tofu Cakes with Chilli Dip 58
tomatoes
Bean & Vegetable Chilli 88
Cherry Tomato, Rosemary & Sea Salt Focaccia 116
Greek Salad Crostini 60
Lentil Bolognese 68
Mediterranean Vegetables with Feta & Olives 78
Mexican Rice 112
Rigatoni with Roast Courgette, Tomato & Mascarpone Sauce 82
Roast Fennel with Cherry Tomatoes & Rosemary 104

vegans 5
Vegetable & Corn Chowder 16
Vegetable Pakoras 30
vegetarian cooking 4–5

walnuts
Avocado Salad with Lime Dressing 38
Blue Cheese & Herb Pâté 26
Caramelized Apple & Blue Cheese Salad 48
Pasta with Two Cheeses & Walnuts 76
White Bean Soup 28
wine
Mixed Nut Roast with Cranberry & Red Wine Sauce 94

yogurt
Mini Roast Vegetable Skewers 22